Advance Praise for
BEYOND HAPPINESS

"Dr. Guttman's book is a game changer. It offers a crystal clear plan on how to transform everyday patterns and lead a more joyful life."

—**Amy B. Scher**, bestselling author of
How To Heal Yourself When No One Else Can

BEYOND HAPPINESS

BEYOND HAPPINESS

The 6 Secrets of Lifetime Satisfaction

DR. JENNIFER GUTTMAN

Post Hill
PRESS

Post Hill Press
New York • Nashville
posthillpress.com

Published in the United States of America
1 2 3 4 5 6 7 8 9 10

For Steven and Alexa.

Without you, my life would not be sustainably satisfied.
It is by your sides that I have learned to be an advocate and an
observer: made and watched decisions being made and faced fears.
This has sometimes been terrifying and sometimes thrilling,
but always satisfying!

Contents

Note from the Author

I am a Doctor of Psychology and bound by doctor-client privilege. All of the stories and examples in this book are true, but the identifying characteristics of my clients have been completely obscured to protect everyone's privacy unless the client has given me written permission to use their story.

This book is not intended to be a replacement for professional advice, diagnosis, or treatment. Please seek the advice of a qualified mental health professional or other health provider with any questions you may have before, during or after reading this book. Never disregard professional advice or delay in seeking it because of something you have read here.

Introduction

People seek me out when things aren't going well in their lives. Hundreds of clients have walked through the door of my psychotherapy office, sat down on the dark-purple leather sofa across from me in significant states of despair, and sought help in navigating mental health challenges, relationships, career changes, or grief. They're discontented, overwhelmed, feeling things aren't as they should be, or unable to navigate or recover from life's inevitable troubles. Their circumstances may vary, but be they artist or executive, high school student or overwhelmed parent, struggling college graduate or retiree, most of them ask me, "Shouldn't I be happy?"

When this happens, my clients need the tools or enough faith in themselves to cope with a problem. They feel paralyzed because they have relinquished or delegated control of their emotions, contentment, and sense of self to external forces, believing there is no other choice. They feel existentially defeated in their efforts not only to effect change in their lives but to thrive.

Maybe you can relate?

I certainly can.

There was one particularly rough-yet-transformational time when my life's path veered and twisted in unexpected ways. A time when I felt I might have given into paralysis and allowed external forces to make choices not just about my happiness, but how I was going to move forward in life. It was during that period I found my way to becoming the therapist—and more important, the human being—I am today. It's when I realized I was looking for the wrong thing—happiness—and that there was something far more important and ultimately sustainable.

My journey began when I was the only one who could see that my infant son was seriously ill.

"I'm surprised he didn't die." That's what the doctor told me.

It was a mother's worst nightmare, right?

Yes and no. Yes, because who would ever wish an illness on their child? No, because my son was a survivor, and finally, after almost nine long years of battling a medical mystery and challenging the experts, we had an answer! And hopefully, a path forward.

From the time my son, Steven, was six months old, he had suffered from a chronic cough and difficulty swallowing his food. Despite my certainty that there was something medically wrong with him, I was consistently turned away by medical professionals, who ascribed his symptoms to asthma, acid reflux, and, eventually, a "psychological" cough. Doctors, friends, and family members all insisted I was imagining more dire health issues than were present, and they passed it off as me being a first-time mom. They felt I should relax and listen to the experts, all subtext for "Behave." I was doing all I could to find ways to face the fear of the unknown and help my child but found myself in a place where I felt like I was free-falling toward hopeless powerlessness.

I spent many unhappy years trying to stave off the internal and external doubt propagated by the people around me. For Steven, those were agonizing years because not only did he want an answer, but he was also so sick so much of the time. He battled two bouts of pneumonia, frequently coughed so violently he'd vomit, visited countless doctors, was treated for maladies he didn't have, and was ridiculed at school for his cough.

Yet all the while, he maintained a sense of humor about it. How did he do that? How did he not curl up in a ball and want to give up? Did we sustain each other with our perseverance and hope?

After an almost nine-year cycle of research and disappointment, I located a children's hospital in Colorado that agreed to look into his case, and we packed our bags and flew there from our home in Westchester County, New York. After a CAT scan, the doctor there saw what all the others had ignored. It was *not* asthma. *Not* reflux. *Not* a psychological cough. And *not* the imaginings of a hysterical first-time mother. In fact, Steven had something called a *double aortic arch*. It's a rare condition, almost always diagnosed before the age of three before permanent damage develops.

What did this condition mean for Steven? Most people are born with one aorta—the large artery that carries blood from your heart to the rest of your body—but Steven was born with *two*. The second had wrapped itself around his trachea and esophagus multiple times, slowly strangling him. That doctor's words will always resonate in my mind: *I'm surprised he didn't die.*

From Colorado, we flew to Boston, where a pediatric cardiac surgeon performed open-heart surgery on my nine-year-old child, cutting and clamping one of his aortas to free up his trachea and esophagus. His windpipe was permanently damaged, but his esophageal symptoms receded.

Besides enduring the ravages to his body, Steven had lost the invincibility and innocence of youth during those years. However, together we learned something about ourselves and each other. We discovered we could spring back from adversity, we could persist and remain positive and hopeful in the face of seemingly insurmountable challenges, and we were united by a bond that made us better able to confront future problems with that same life satisfaction and resilience. We'd discovered something beyond happiness.

As I thought about all we'd endured, I wondered, *How could I share this lesson in resilience to help other people so they could sustain a life of satisfaction?*

But before I could think this through, things in my life got worse.

* * *

At a family party to celebrate Steven's eleventh birthday, I began to feel short of breath. My shortness of breath turned into terrible chest pain and increasing difficulty breathing. So as not to alarm my family, I left the restaurant and went to sit in my car, hoping the discomfort would subside and I could return to the party. Reclining the seat made things worse, and I started to get really frightened—*something wasn't right*. A family member came to check on me. By that time, catching my breath was so difficult that forming words was nearly impossible. Because there was no time to wait for an ambulance, my family drove me to the emergency department. I distinctly remember not wanting my children to see me die as I tried to reassure them with my eyes that I was going to be okay.

A CAT scan revealed multiple pulmonary embolisms. One of them was lodged between two ribs, causing the terrible pain. Miraculously, it was the pain that had saved my life. Without it, I wouldn't have known something was wrong, and the embolisms could have traveled to my heart or brain.

After a week of medical observation and blood thinners, I was released from the hospital. During my recovery, I had the opportunity to reflect. We are only on this planet one time, and that time is fleeting. While facing my fear of death, I had been so worried my children would be left without a mother. I wanted to make sure I made the most of my years with them. I also resolved not to let fear inhibit or prevent me from whatever I might be able to make of my life. I decided to use it to motivate myself to embrace every possibility. I vowed to lead a proactive life, and I realized that *having a purpose, no matter how daunting, would help me maintain hope*. I also realized that whatever I wanted to accomplish as a mother and a psychologist needed to be done now—not later, because later *is* now.

I just had to figure out *how*.

* * *

It's inevitable—life will throw us curveballs, sometimes several at a time. Before I'd made much progress pushing forward, my father passed away. I was blindsided once again. Years of facing Steven's frightening-yet-nameless illness, open-heart surgery on a *nine-year-old*, my near-death experience, and now this—it was such a concentration of uncertainty, fear, and sorrow in a very short period of time. I don't want to minimize the grief of people who lose their parents at a much younger age, but for me, it had been a lot of blows, one after another, without much recovery time in between.

After my father's funeral, I made a decision to take three weeks off from work—an unprecedented amount of time for me. But I had to do *something*—I'd been in a state of perpetual stress for almost fourteen years. This decision was not a popular one among a lot of the people in my life, who thought I was running away from my problems, but my kids (who were at sleepaway camp) and their father were supportive, so I resisted the urge to people please and did what felt authentically right for me. I packed a carry-on, flew to Europe on my own, and traveled without much of an agenda. I made a conscious decision to redirect my energy into a renewed sense of strength and positivity and find a path forward.

I needed the brain space to figure out how to regain my sense of purpose, optimism, and hope. In some ways, I went looking for happiness, but I couldn't help but wonder if there was something more. I gave myself the gift of time to mourn my father and get my head straight. I knew I had to move on from my solitary grief phase and integrate what I'd learned. All my life experiences could hold me back, keep me paralyzed by fear of more fear, illness, death, and grief, *or* I could learn something of value from them.

I decided to go with the latter. It was during this time that I came to see that happiness isn't enough and that we need something beyond it—something that keeps us moving forward when we get that bad news, when our kids are sick, when we lose a job, when it feels like our troubles will never end. Something that can help us stay the course on a bad day or even a bad year. I realized that happiness isn't the ultimate goal—it's a great feeling but not the endgame—satisfaction is. That's when the idea of Sustainable Life Satisfaction took root.

As I traveled, I thought about who I was during each of my challenging experiences. How had I behaved? How had I dealt with challenges? How had I responded to adversity? How had I responded to being misunderstood? What had made me so... well...*resilient?*

I realized that even in the worst circumstances, I had an embedded ability to intuitively problem-solve, investigate until I found solutions, and bounce back in order to implement them. That's what had gotten me through the tough times and kept me going. I thought this must be the source of my resilience—what kept me empowered and hopeful even when I wasn't "feeling" particularly happy.

But there was more to it than that....

I have never been a person who blindly follows the rules—if an authority figure tells me to do something, I don't always listen. If a doctor advises me to stay in bed for a week, I probably won't; if friends tell me I shouldn't work on weekends or see so many clients, I'm likely to ignore them; if someone tells me that traveling to a certain country has health risks, I plan accordingly, but go; I've never been a person who gives up, no matter the odds.

Am I oppositional? Just plain hardheaded?

Oppositional doesn't feel quite right because I'm not doing it to intentionally challenge another person or their beliefs.

Defiant is more like it! I am defiant in the face of the obstacles that I believe I can overcome.

And maybe it's defiance that helped me listen to what everybody had to say, analyze and curate it, keep what felt authentically right, and discard what didn't. Maybe that's what helped me stand up to doctors for Steven, or to my friends and family when I needed time for self-care. Putting the pieces together, I had an epiphany: I'm *defiantly resilient*. Being defiantly resilient is a state beyond happiness, achieved through Sustainable Life Satisfaction. That is the goal—not the feeling of happiness.

* * *

Defiant resilience is the ability to spring back from adversity with a belief in your authentic problem-solving skills, to face challenges head-on with self-generated strength and positivity. This characteristic develops when we navigate and survive difficult times, increasing our sense of purpose and giving us hope to face whatever challenges lie ahead. When difficult circumstances knock you down (and they will), defiant resilience is what allows you to get up and move through and past them while continuing to thrive and live your life sustainably satisfied—beyond the fleeting feelings of happiness.

I call it *defiant* resilience because, often in life, there will be people who think they have all the answers or know what is best for you, and ultimately, you will have to act, based not on what they are advising, but what the voice inside of you is saying—like I did when Steven received the diagnosis of "psychological cough" over and over again from doctors. It is not that I was *against* those doctors, but I was *for* my son. I heard what the experts had to say, assessed the information, and discarded what didn't seem right, never deafening myself to my beliefs.

Remember, even if there are no naysayers to defy, when you are resilient, you are defying the adversity itself. You are saying, "Yes, this is painful, but I still choose to live *my* truth fully." You are able to thrive during the sad, painful, and complicated days, as well as the happy ones.

Understanding this was what kept me going despite those dubious doctors, my pulmonary embolisms, fear, and grief. My awareness of this led to a renewed sense of purpose. I wanted to explore and delineate this and share what I'd learned with others. I wanted to do something *intentional*—something more than sitting in my office and talking to people.

I had found my purpose: I'd guide my clients to a sustainably satisfied life—to a life beyond happiness!

* * *

I began to explore the factors that had glued me together and helped me move forward even in the worst of times. If I could map those out, I could share my strategy.

That's how Sustainable Life Satisfaction was conceived.

I realized there was a through line of techniques that had carried me across all the traumatic events of the past years. If defiant resilience is the final and crucial component of an empowered life, the key to sustainable satisfaction, how do we get there? As I thought about all I'd gone through, I noticed some patterns. I had consistently done six things:

1. I avoided assumptions.
2. I reduced people-pleasing behavior.
3. I faced my fears.

4. I made decisions.
5. I followed through and became a closer.
6. I actively self-reinforced.

Here's how it worked in my life:

I avoided assumptions about what was wrong with Steven based solely on doctors' incomplete opinions about the cause of his illness. Likewise, I didn't assume that if I had been gravely ill once with pulmonary embolisms, I should consider myself fragile and proceed with more caution in life than I authentically felt was necessary.

I reduced people-pleasing behavior by never accepting the doctors' assumptions about Steven's health. By not people pleasing, I kept myself from becoming complacent and didn't allow others to reduce my advocacy or negatively affect my tenacity. I challenged the experts, argued with friends. And I went against the advice of family members. I didn't give in, no matter how uncomfortable it made other people. There were so many times when I wondered if I should keep looking for answers, but I pushed on despite the outside interference and negativity. I didn't people please by allowing others' assumptive fears about my potentially fragile health after my embolisms to deter me, despite the loving place their concern came from. Likewise, when friends and family didn't want me to go to Europe for three weeks, I followed my internal and authentic path despite pressure to remain at home to mourn.

Next...I faced my fears. If you've ever had a chronically ill child, you know how terrifying it can be. For years, I'd wake up every morning and face my dread of the unknown. By refusing to believe the doctors' diagnoses, I forced myself to find the truth.

I confronted my fear of authority figures by standing up to and challenging doctors—*lots* of doctors. Later, instead of reverting to a state of self-protective defense and stagnation, I continued to face my fears by choosing to move forward after enduring illness and grief.

Then...I made decisions and committed to them. Should I accept a diagnosis that doesn't make sense? Which doctor should I take Steven to next—a gastroenterologist or a pulmonologist? Should I send him to sleepaway camp or not? Is it worthwhile to travel all the way to Colorado? Each step of the way, I had to make decisions. And this continued after having suffered the pulmonary embolisms. Was it safe to fly in an airplane? What medications should I take? Could I remain true to my love of adventure and manage the health risks? Ultimately, these were questions only I could answer.

And as I did...I followed through and became a closer. I didn't stop until I had answers, until I'd securely closed the door on this hard chapter in our lives. I can't tell you how many times I promised Steven, "I'm going to knock down every door until we have a resolution." Likewise, I decided that, going forward, I would travel to the far reaches of the world despite having suffered pulmonary embolisms—and I have, starting when I went to Europe for three weeks.

Throughout the entire process, I actively self-reinforced. I took care of myself even when the path with Steven was hard. Sometimes, this meant a good cry in the shower; sometimes, it meant going to see a movie or play to get out of my head for a few hours. I self-reinforced after my father passed away by giving myself permission to take care of my needs by leaving for a few weeks to grieve.

* * *

Each of these techniques helped me cope with the unforeseen challenges and events I encountered. However, when combined… when *synthesized*…they gave me the self-empowerment, fortitude, and determination to persevere.

As I began to teach these skills to my clients, I saw something incredible happen over and over again! As people consistently applied my Sustainable Life Satisfaction techniques, *they* were not only becoming more satisfied and resilient, but they were also realizing that happiness isn't the goal—it's a feeling.

It took time, motivation, and patience, but they developed the capacity to rebound and transcend, not only from ordinary, everyday problems—a traffic jam that made them miss a big meeting, a child struggling with schoolwork, an argument with their partner—but also the gut punches that can cause lasting pain, like divorce, injury, illness, injustice, or the death of a loved one. Bad stuff will happen—there's no avoiding it—but we can choose to make it a path forward, a path toward hope, *and nobody is exempt from possibility.*

My wish for you is that the path of Sustainable Life Satisfaction will be your road map to *your* best opportunities, to *your* life of defiant resilience: beyond happiness.

CHAPTER 1

An Epidemic of Existential Despair

Before I show you how to understand, navigate, and implement the techniques of Sustainable Life Satisfaction, I need to make something very clear: it's no accident I use the word *satisfaction* and not *happiness*. This is because our ideas about happiness are misguided.

My client Andrea taught me this beautifully.

A few years ago, a young woman came to my office and sat down on that purple leather couch. If you were to go by Andrea's appearance, you might not have guessed how much she was struggling. She was tall and pretty, with long hair and warm brown eyes. She embodied an effortless elegance—not flashy, but subtle, tasteful, and comfortable. She was impressively poised for a college student home on winter break from her first year at UCLA. It wasn't until she began telling me about her life that it became apparent how miserable she was.

Like a lot of people her age, Andrea scripted entire narratives about herself and the people in her life via social media, which she scrutinized and analyzed many times a day. When she saw online that someone was having a party to which her friends were invited and she was not, she became disproportionately insecure and depressed. When she texted someone and didn't hear back instantly, she assumed that not only were they mad at her, but they were spending time with other friends, *better* friends, and saying negative things about her. Andrea knew she consistently came across as defensive, clingy, sad, and moody, and she wanted people to reach out and inquire about what was troubling her. When they didn't, she was hurt.

Toward the end of our first conversation, Andrea asked the question so many of my clients in their late teens and early twenties ask: "Why am I so unhappy?"

Although my older clients experience different types of circumstances and situations as the source of their troubles, they, too, struggle against unhappiness. They have all lost their sense of purpose, of joy and wonder in life, and they often feel undeserving of what successes they have. In this era of anxiety about economics, politics, climate, and health, this shared despair is growing worse. I'd go so far as to say there is *an epidemic of existential despair* in this country and beyond, and that is because people in every demographic persist in chasing a false idea of *happiness*.

I encounter clients like this every day—people crippled by a core sense of inadequacy, imposter syndrome, and self-loathing colliding with an impossible standard. "I should be happy...I want to be happy...I have read all the happiness books...I even meditate and do yoga! Why is it I'm still not happy?"

Such a good question.

After I returned home from my soul-searching trip to Europe, I hunted for answers in a lot of places. I spent hours upon hours in bookstores and bought all the bestsellers my clients were reading. I watched a lot of TED Talks. I listened to every sort of podcast you can imagine. I followed the leading happiness "experts" on social media and tried to understand as much as I could about their approaches, but something still felt off. I could not reconcile all the happiness advice out there with my goal for my clients: a *sustainable*, unflappable belief in their inherent worthiness and lovability.

Then, it came to me: *our society is setting people up on a quest for failure because striving to feel sustainably happy is the wrong goal.* Happiness is a fleeting emotion, an endorphin rush, a chemical high. It is the moment the text message comes in, when the boss says yes, the first kiss, a picture on Instagram that tells only part of the story. It is *not* the foundation for a life of contentment. It does not equip us with the skills of resilience (defiant and otherwise) we need to navigate the challenges that are every person's reality, especially during the really hard times—like when our lives have been upended by a pandemic and the ensuant disruption and fear, fractured by politics and the social and racial tensions that ripple through our communities, or whenever "normal" seems an impossible goal and happiness even more so.

I began to understand that feeling happy is an aspiration, not a reliable result. *Satisfaction*, on the other hand, is an achievable and sustainable goal. As I applied these theories to my practice, it became startlingly clear: Sustainable Life Satisfaction encompasses the behavioral techniques that take my clients from being deeply unhappy, depressed, or anxious people who feel inherently unlovable and who are living in a state of existential despair to being highly functional and deeply fulfilled. The best part is that mastering Sustainable Life Satisfaction does not require in-person soul-baring with a therapist. These are practices anyone can do here and now to change how they think, feel, and, ultimately, how they live.

The six fundamental techniques—avoiding assumptions, reducing people pleasing, facing fears, making decisions, closing, and self-reinforcing—are all easy to learn. And when you start applying them, you will feel relief right away. With consistent practice, you will achieve cognitive optimization, which means rewiring your brain to function in a new, more efficient, more effective way.

Exactly who do you think you are?

In other words, what's your self-concept?

A clear and empowered self-concept is one outcome of implementing the Sustainable Life Satisfaction techniques. Without knowing and trusting everything that's strong, reliable, and authentic about yourself, you can't move forward. In other words, without an empowered self-concept, without knowing and trusting who you are, you can't come anywhere close to *anybody's* definition of happiness or satisfaction.

I believe an empowered self-concept includes five elements:

First is self-worth. This means having faith in your significance in the world, trusting in your value as a human being, and not delegating the reinforcement of that value to others.

Then comes self-confidence. This is a belief in your ability to cope with your thoughts and feelings so they don't interfere with your ability to complete your goals. Any of them—easy or hard, short term or long term.

Self-efficacy comes next. This is your belief in your problem-solving and coping skills. It's an overall feeling of competency. It helps you see that you can handle life's challenges. With self-efficacy comes a belief in your agency to influence the events in your life as opposed to being at the mercy of them. This is called having an *internal locus of control* and is empowering.

Self-efficacy leads to self-respect. You'll notice that you are consistently achieving a standard of behavior commensurate with your capacities and capabilities; you'll respect yourself no matter what other people say or how they try to challenge your sense of self.

Belief in your inherent lovability is the final part of an empowered self-concept. You trust that you are lovable even when the people in your life oppose the actions you take to achieve self-empowerment. You believe that those people will stay around—even when you do things they may not like or when you do not serve them or live your life for them—*because* you are a lovable person. Acknowledging your lovability will transcend even the potential loss of someone who does not support your journey to becoming your most authentic self, living a life of equanimity beyond happiness.

Think about these five elements of an empowered self-concept—self-worth, self-confidence, self-efficacy, self-respect, and belief in your inherent lovability. Did you notice that "Learning to control *outcomes*" is not on the list? That is because all five are about assuming control of the only thing you can control in this world: *yourself*. Even though it feels far safer for us to believe we can affect outcomes that were never ours to direct in the first place, as you master the techniques of Sustainable Life Satisfaction, you'll see that giving up the fantasy that you have total power over anything besides yourself—your child's behavior, your partner's reactions, your coworker's moods, politics, crises, or the world in general—is a key part of self-empowerment. Every other thing in your life falls within the "*illusion* of control" category.

What *is* in your control is how you see yourself and the actions in your life that you execute and complete.

An unempowered life is the *opposite* of a satisfied one....

This fantasy of control leads to frustration, disappointment, self-doubt, anger, and numerous other diminishing, distracting, and sometimes destructive emotions. Giving up the illusion of control may be frightening at first, but as you'll see, when you focus only on what is within your control, you'll allow for confidence and self-empowerment to take root and grow.

For example, there is no place for confidence in a thought like, *If my best friend is invited to a party, it goes to follow that I will be invited too*. This is not an outcome you can control.

In the same way, thoughts like, *If someone cares about me, they will always text me back within an hour* or *My extended family must approve of my decisions and actions* are unreasonable because the outcomes are not within your sphere of control and sow the seeds for feelings of disempowerment. Likewise, also unreasonable are scenarios such as *My child's success in school is the only way to prove I am a good parent* or *If I am kept on at my job after a round of layoffs, it will show everyone that I am a valued employee and good at what I do* or *If I am agreeable and compliant and make them feel like I am putting their needs before mine, my partner will never leave me.*

Anything that requires external validation as part of your definition of life satisfaction is the direct route to unhappiness and existential despair.

After working with many clients, I have come to see that the fifth component of an empowered self-concept—the belief in one's inherent lovability—is the key to battling any level of existential despair. Not just when it comes to relationships, but also in careers, parenting, and general well-being. People tend not to talk about this. There is seldom much conversation about how vulnerable it feels or how powerful it might be to say, "This is all that I am. This is all that I have to offer," and believe somebody would want to be around *you*—flaws and all—just for *you*.

It is something you rarely read about in the happiness literature or hear about on social media, where validation tends to come from outside of ourselves. Perhaps this is because a genuine belief in one's inherent lovability is harder to achieve than you might think.

This makes me think of a client of mine who had been in a relationship for a couple of years. On paper, it looked great—Julia loved her job as an architect, and Raphael was an up-and-coming filmmaker. They were interesting people, leading full lives, but as the relationship progressed, Raphael became overly focused on Julia, and his self-efficacy, his trust in his competency, and his agency to manage the events in his life diminished.

It grew more and more clear that Raphael valued their relationship more than he valued himself. Because of this, Julia felt like he was losing himself, his career was suffering as a result, and he was beginning to live his life disproportionately for her. Julia did not want that, not for herself or for Raphael. She explained this to him on many occasions—that she didn't need such overwhelming attention—and encouraged him to follow his opportunities. But he could not hear her, perhaps because, despite the attention he received for his work, he lacked self-confidence and an inherent sense of self-worth. Julia could not get him to see that being in service to her and striving to make her life easier, while sacrificing who he was, was not fostering their relationship. In fact, it seemed to be alarmingly close to becoming a kind of frantic attachment or overattachment.

Julia tried to communicate her feelings, saying, "Go, make movies. That is who you are. You can't live *for* me. Just like I can't live for you." But it was not getting through. Raphael was insulted because his idea of a relationship was defined by all sorts of codependent concepts—a deep-rooted need to be needed. Ultimately, Julia dreaded that this imbalance would lead to them resenting each other, so she ended it with him, saying, "Between running my architecture firm and showing up for my elderly parents, I do not have the mindshare for this—it is not a dynamic I can sustain. Please go do *you*."

They did not speak for almost two years. Julia dated other people, but she still really cared about Raphael, so she reached out. And guess what? His career had taken off! The dreams he had deferred on her behalf when they were a couple had come true. Raphael had missed Julia as well. Now, they are back together, and because Julia applied the Sustainable Life Satisfaction techniques to her relationship and gave Raphael the space (and perhaps a nudge) to take action to experience and realize his self-worth—building confidence, efficacy, self-respect, and a belief in *his* inherent lovability—Julia and Raphael now have a balanced, thriving, and *sustainable* relationship.

Are you beginning to see a pattern? The five elements of self-concept culminate in inherent lovability for a reason. When people first hear the term, they say, "But I already feel inherently lovable." And I always ask, "*Really?* Do you? Do you really feel like all your behaviors reflect your belief that people aren't going to abandon you?" I am certain that if we dig into this, we will uncover the inherent fear that everybody in our lives has the potential to abandon us and that we consequently begin to develop behaviors—like always putting ourselves last or giving too much help or advice—that we are engaging in to make sure that people do not leave. (Remember Raphael and Julia?) The strength, the actual liberation that comes from connecting with your inherent lovability and realizing that people will stay around for you—not because of what you give to or do for them, but just for you—is huge!

As a clinical psychologist, my mission is to help people like Julia and Raphael realize this kind of inherent lovability and life satisfaction, which is dependent on nobody but ourselves to sustain. Without those five elements of empowered self-concept, we feel like we are at the mercy of the world. But when you realize these, you are going to become a person who feels and *is* more resourceful and empowered. It is not that one of the steps of Sustainable Life Satisfaction—such as facing fears or avoiding assumptions—is what makes you sustainably satisfied; it is that these techniques coalesce, and, together, they enable you to have positive feelings about yourself, which *then* enables you to become sustainably satisfied. It is important to understand that when a positive self-concept allows you to feel inherently lovable, *that* is what ultimately is the foundation of Sustainable Life Satisfaction.

How do we go beyond happiness?

How does a person get to a place where they consistently embody an empowered self-concept?

The answer is through *action*—living well and directing our energies toward finding the sustainable and satisfied life that is midway between excess and deficiency, between narcissism and neediness. That is why the six Sustainable Life Satisfaction techniques are all practical and active—they are not conceptual. They are things you can train yourself to *do*, naturally and consistently, to live a good life and appreciate and support the people and the world around you instead of relying on external influences and factors for your inner calm and joy. These six tools will liberate you from wasting your time, and ultimately, your life, trying to control circumstances that are out of your reach and allow you to focus on what you can control—your own reactions and behavior—for a life beyond happiness, a place of defiant resilience.

I'll go into lots of detail later, but let's start with an overview of the six fundamental behaviors embedded in Sustainable Life Satisfaction.

First of all, you avoid assumptions....

By avoiding assumptions, you can learn to have agency in any situation *instead* of taking action based on what you imagine other people are thinking or feeling about you. Instead, your actions are based on reliable evidence. Note that this is an *action* technique—because your actions in any given situation will not be motivated by assumptions but by hard facts or, at the very least, really good guesses. As you avoid assumptions and engage in realistic, evidence-based thinking, you will build self-confidence and self-efficacy.

The second step is reducing people-pleasing behaviors....

What I mean by "people-pleasing behaviors" is subordinating and conforming your needs, desires, wishes, and dreams to what other people think they should be—or to what you *imagine* others want them to be. This technique of consciously not defaulting to putting the needs and desires of others ahead of your own enables you to live an authentic life.

Authenticity means paying attention to and acting on your own wishes, desires, and dreams. It means you are freeing yourself from doing things for the purpose of securing feelings of indispensability—like doing things because you are scared people will abandon you. Not only will this lead to genuine, more meaningful connections, but it ultimately fosters self-worth and a genuine belief in your inherent lovability.

Step three is facing your fears....

The purpose of the facing-fears technique is not to stop you from feeling afraid—after all, some fear is healthy—it is to train you not to let your fears prevent you from working toward and achieving your goals. You can learn to use your fears as a positive motivation that propels you to move toward the life you want, resulting in more self-efficacy and self-respect.

The fourth step is making decisions....

Using this technique, you will liberate yourself to make choices by recognizing that almost every decision we settle on is, at best, just a well-informed guess and that there are almost no decisions that cannot be reversed. Of course, there are a few exceptions—like having a child or a financial gamble that results in an irrevocable loss—but when it comes to the day-to-day, most decisions—like which college to go to or whether to move to a new city—can be undone. The point is to take action and *make* a decision. When you do, you will experience more self-confidence and self-efficacy.

With the fifth step, closing, you acknowledge that starting is easy, but finishing is hard....

This truism teaches the skill of following through and completing tasks, from small ones that will make your life easier—like folding and putting away laundry or paying your bills on time—to large ones that can change your life—like starting a new business, buying a home, or ending a destructive relationship. Following through on what we start, *no matter* how difficult the process, will lead to self-confidence, self-efficacy, and self-respect.

Finally, self-reinforce by rewarding yourself for putting all the Sustainable Life Satisfaction techniques into practice....

This enables you to stay on the path to belief in your inherent lovability. As you consistently provide yourself with tangible rewards for successfully executing any of the other five techniques, you will make the cognitive shift from aspiring to gain and needing praise, rewards, and reassurance from others to appreciating the profound value of giving those things to yourself.

Note that the rewards you give yourself should be concrete. I often buy myself theater tickets—we're talking orchestra seats—when I have closed a given set of tasks that I have set for myself during the week. One of my clients really likes popcorn from street vendors or movie theaters and considers it an out-of-the-ordinary delight, so when they successfully complete any of techniques one through five, they go out and buy some popcorn.

I cannot overstate the importance of giving your brain a reward for doing the tough work of successfully enacting the other five Sustainable Life Satisfaction techniques. If you don't, it is natural to think, *This is hard stuff—why should I keep doing it?* But as you reward yourself, you will start to develop, and ultimately retain, all five qualities.

These six fundamental techniques are the essence of moving beyond happiness....

I will go into more detail about each one, giving real-life examples of how my clients have used them to empower themselves, and share my best how-to-do-this instructions so that you can apply them to your life and situations and practice and become proficient in them—*all of them; you can't cherry-pick!* And as you grow into a sense of defiant resilience, you will come to recognize that some things deep within you have irrevocably changed.

But remember that to reach the kind of self-empowerment I have dedicated myself to helping my clients achieve in their lives, it will be necessary for you to use all six of these techniques simultaneously. If you think, *Well, I am pretty good at closing, but I could really use help with my people-pleasing behavior*, it is fine to jump to the chapter about people pleasing and listen to that first, but make sure you go back and work with all the techniques because, ultimately, they are intertwined and inseparable.

I put the Sustainable Life Satisfaction techniques in the order I did for a reason. As you will come to see, avoiding assumptions and reducing people-pleasing behaviors come first because they are necessary steps in allowing you to face your fears and authentically make decisions about what to close on. Active self-reinforcement of these behaviors guides your journey through Sustainable Life Satisfaction to that place beyond happiness, a place of defiant resilience.

Practiced together, the techniques will help you live a life in which self-worth, self-confidence, self-efficacy, self-respect, and a belief in your inherent lovability become ingrained elements of your character. Like my clients, you will experience how you can make meaningful, positive changes and empower yourself to live a life of sustainable satisfaction, where happiness is a wonderful feeling but never the ultimate goal.

Let's start with avoiding assumptions.

CHAPTER 2

Where Is the Evidence?

Avoiding Assumptions

I like to say that fear is *consistently opting for worst-case assumptions.*

The connection to negative forecasting—expecting that undesirable things will happen—is clear. But there are many guesses and predictions based on incomplete information we make on an ongoing basis that diminish our opportunities for satisfaction. These are things like imagining what other people *may* think or feel about us, what we assume an outcome *may* be in a situation, or our fantasies or anxieties about what *might* happen.

Assuming means anticipating what another person is going to say or do (usually something detrimental to you), convincing yourself that your belief about what will happen is true and then preemptively trying to solve a problem that does not actually exist yet. In other words, assumptions are guesses or predictions based on a little bit of information but not necessarily all of it.

Research conducted by Bojana Kuzmanovic of the Max Planck Institute in Cologne reported that we look for information that supports our beliefs because when we find it, we receive a reinforcing boost. Even when we are 99 percent wrong, the brain looks for the 1 percent so that it can say, "Hey, you were right about this decision." That's why our beliefs are so difficult to shift—the brain loves to be correct. It wants to give us the equivalent of an adrenaline rush, even when we are wrong.

Clearly, the trouble with assumptions is that far too often, they are incorrect. When we take action based on erroneous information, we are setting ourselves up for toxic situations. Making decisions based on guessing instead of facts is a dangerous exercise. But when we begin to stop assuming, we nurture all our Sustainable Life Satisfaction qualities, especially self-concept and self-respect.

As with all the techniques, *intent* must be followed by *execution*, just as *thought* must be reinforced by *action*. It is important to bear in mind that avoiding assumptions is a *behavior*, not merely a way of thinking. *Consciously* taking steps toward evaluating information is a decision to walk through the fear that is created by waiting for an outcome, and when we do, we develop and sustain the patience to pause until something tangible occurs. But this happens *only* if or when we have all the evidence, which is what makes avoiding assumptions an action solution.

Ask yourself: Would my assumption hold up in court?

Whenever you make a decision or take an action based on someone else's behaviors or intentions, it is a good idea to ask yourself, "Do I have *factual* evidence?"

Another way to look at it is: What would be admissible in a court of law? Could I convince a jury made up of twelve of my peers?

Facts are *not* a facial expression, a conjecture, someone else's subjective opinion, past experiences with another person, a story that happened to go viral, or body language. Only unequivocal actions and words will stand up in court. You need proof. Attempts to read nonverbal cues as a means of social communication can be ineffective and even dangerous. Our responses to them are tainted by our experiences, overexposure to digital media with concurrent social isolation, filters, and Photoshop, all of which have impacted our discernment.

Remember at the beginning of the chapter when I said that avoiding assumptions is based on actions and not thoughts? This is what I mean—weigh the physical, verbal evidence.

Unless there is physical or verbal evidence of a thought or action from another person, you will likely be operating based on a projection of your own past experiences onto the new situation. And you will probably also be taking action based on that past experience because—even if it is unhealthy or destructive—that's more comfortable than the fear that arises when you do not know what another person is thinking or what they will do and how their behavior will affect you.

How do we learn to make assumptions?

As children, we desperately want to make our parents proud. From an early age, we start guessing about how they might think or respond to us, and we adjust our behavior based on that guesswork. A toddler might be praised for keeping quiet, being "seen and not heard," and consequently learn not to express their feelings. A teenager might be told how attractive they are when they have lost a little weight and then adjust their diet to garner further compliments. When parents give us positive feedback, we value it—it is a reward.

However, it can be more subtle than that—a child can be reinforced for making an incorrect assumption. For example, if a parent is in a bad mood and the child stays in their room to please the parent and is then reinforced for that consideration, the child feels emboldened by their "magical" powers to "read" moods. Bolstered by our sense of how good we *think* we are at what can often be maladaptive behavior, we grow up and head out into the world, where we attempt to repeat the behaviors for which our parents praised us in our interpersonal relationships. This is frequently an attempt to protect ourselves from or reduce the potential for emotional pain.

A child whose parents were inconsistent in their relationship with them might grow into an adult who believes, *I am going to break up with my partner because I know they're going to break up with me.* A child who is silenced or ignored may grow into an adult who thinks, *Nobody listens to me anyway, and since my opinions don't matter, what's the point of speaking up?*

These are great examples of *social learning theory*. Psychologist Albert Bandura developed the concept. He believed that we learn from each other via imitation, modeling, and observation. We adjust our behaviors and reactions as they are reinforced, especially by our caregivers during childhood. If your parent punished or belittled you for something you did, you were less likely to repeat that behavior, but if you were praised for an action, you would likely repeat it to please them.

The impact of social learning theory was highlighted for me while working in a residential facility for convicted adolescent girls. I used a group anger-control treatment with them in the hopes of reducing their sentences. Role-playing was conducted between me and a co-leader, and then the girls followed our lead. In accordance with Bandura's theory, the girls responded well to the modeling and imitation, as well as the praise and feedback they received from me after their participation.

When it comes to our daily lives, social learning theory demonstrates that whenever you come into a situation with a lot of baggage, with a lot of assumptions, you are reading a situation based on your own history and not taking into account the true circumstances of that situation or the actual experiences of the person with whom you are interacting.

Take my client Taylor for example. She had a self-defeating habit in her romantic relationships: she was a serial cheater. She cheated because she assumed her boyfriends would cheat on *her*, so it was better to inoculate herself against the pain by cheating first. The reason she was sure her boyfriends were going to cheat was that *her* mother had cheated on her father, broken up their marriage, and proceeded to cheat on all her subsequent romantic partners.

Although not commendable, Taylor's behavior is understandable—it clearly derived from her social learning environment. Her self-concept most likely took a hit as well—witnessing all that unfaithfulness modeled feelings of unworthiness, as if she could never be enough for a romantic partner. And, in turn, her unfaithfulness was disappointing, and sometimes heartbreaking, for the guys she dated, not to mention for herself. This was not a recipe for Sustainable Life Satisfaction. In fact, it was making her miserable.

Taylor came to each new relationship with baggage. In other words, she saw other people through the lens of painful events in her history. Although seemingly natural to Taylor because of her early influences and past experiences, this way of behaving without facts is counterintuitive—a person whom you have just met and begun dating has had no role in that history. Each of Taylor's romantic partners may or may not have had an inclination to be unfaithful to her, but because she grew up with parents who couldn't *not* be unfaithful to each other or anyone else, she assumed that everyone always cheats.

Whether they are aware of it or not, people like Taylor make assumptions in this way because it gives them the illusion of control over their lives. The pattern is illusory because what they are attempting to control—*before it even happens*—is someone else's behavior. The thought might be, *You are going to cheat on me, and I will stop you from doing that by cheating on you first*, or *I know I am going to fail, so I might as well quit*. But what really happens is that every time you act on a negative assumption like this, you are sending yourself the implicit message: *I do not have the patience to wait and see how this person will actually behave or how circumstances will unfold because I won't know how to manage a problem if it actually arises*. When stuck in a mindset like this, there is no possibility of having a positive outcome or arriving at the ultimate goal of Sustainable Life Satisfaction.

That's what we call a *thinking error*.

What do I mean by that?

A thinking error is the gap between a thought about a situation and the reality of the situation itself.

Thinking errors are one of the key concepts of cognitive-behavioral therapy, or CBT, upon which the Sustainable Life Satisfaction techniques are based. Understanding them will help with avoiding assumptions and all the Sustainable Life Satisfaction steps. Cognitive-behavioral psychologists note that people are prone to committing thinking errors, those maladaptive thought processes that erode our self-worth, self-confidence, self-efficacy, and self-respect. These thoughts do not represent a true picture of events and circumstances but instead project a negative, distorted picture that the person *believes* to be true. For example, a student fails one test, so they believe that they are terrible at all tests or, worse, a failure in general.

In fact, thinking errors cause a good deal of the world's suffering—with misperceptions and breakdowns in communication leading to all sorts of conflicts. The core of CBT is a set of techniques—reality checks, if you will—to correct these thinking errors as they arise, thus significantly ameliorating the difficult moods that are inseparable from them. In CBT terms, the four major types of thinking errors or cognitive distortions are negative forecasting, all-or-none thinking, magnification, and minimization.

If we examine them closely, we will see that they are inextricable from not only how we regulate our moods and emotions but also how we effectively live our lives, as well as all the assumptions involved in the process.

Let's start with negative forecasting....

This is also known as *fortune-telling*. It means predicting and expecting terrible things to happen—it's the most blatant kind of assuming. For example, *I have been laid off, and I will never find another job.* The flaw in this forecasting thought is that a part of your mind is occupied with losing your job and all its ramifications, which induces anxiety and leaves you with less mindshare or bandwidth to devote to the task of revising your résumé, reaching out to contacts, and going on interviews—doing the work to find a new job. The negative forecasting interferes with your ability to act on whatever it is you want or need to do and becomes a self-fulfilling prophecy. We ruminate disproportionately on these faulty negative assumptions more so than on positive or neutral ones, setting us on the path to existential despair.

I'll share an example of all-or-none thinking....

"I always get lost," Milo lamented one day as he slumped on my purple couch in a posture of utter defeat.

"Really?" I replied. "Then, how did you get to my office today?"

He looked at me skeptically.

I continued, "If you always got lost, like you just said, you would not be here right now. You also would not be able to find your way home when you leave. Maybe you don't have the best sense of direction. But be careful what words you use to describe yourself, even in your thoughts, because your brain never stops listening. 'I always get lost' sends a message of alarm to your brain every time you have to get from point A to point B, and your brain will activate your sympathetic nervous system, making it *more* likely you'll get lost."

I hear statements like Milo's from clients all the time. And it is not just the everyday stuff like always getting lost. It is things like, "I am never going to meet someone, and I'm going to die alone," or "My family will always keep me from living the kind of life I've dreamed of." These assumptions are all so self-defeating, and there is no evidence that negative thinking can help with any situation, large or small.

A clue that you are engaging in all-or-none thinking is when you find yourself using superlatives—words like *always*, *never*, *best*, or *worst*—to describe yourself or your situation to other people or even to yourself inside your head. All-or-none thinking, like negative forecasting, impedes or diverts you from achieving your desired goal and thus from Sustainable Life Satisfaction. All-or-none thinking eliminates the gray area between rigid absolutes; however, life is lived in the gray area.

Magnification is a heartbeat away from negative forecasting and all-or-none thinking....

With magnification, your brain looks for and filters in negative events instead of balancing positive events appropriately against the negative ones. Magnification is making a small, undesirable event very big in your mind; it is blowing something minor completely out of proportion to the reality of the situation.

Let's say you have a performance review at work. You are being evaluated in eight aspects of your job on a scale of one to five, where a one is "unsatisfactory" and a five is "exceptional." Imagine you get mostly fours ("exceeds expectations") and fives, and your overall rating is a four, but there was a single two ("needs improvement") in the mix. If you are someone who magnifies, you will focus on the two, and ignore the reality that your overall rating was "exceeds expectations." You might think something like, "I got a two! My boss thinks I am the worst. Now I will never get that year-end bonus—let alone the promotion I was hoping for."

And of course, the inverse of magnification is minimization....

Minimization is when you ignore or mentally reduce the significance of positive events or feedback. In the example of the performance review, the same person who magnifies the two rating minimizes all the fours and fives, as well as the overall "exceeds expectations" evaluation, making the "needs improvement" more glaring.

I once worked with a client named Danny, who had a face many people found compellingly handsome. At 5'4", he was also shorter than most men. He *hated* being short—he considered it a personal defect. He received lots of compliments for his looks, and his reflexive habit was to dismiss the praise because his external asset—his face—hardly mattered to him when measured against what he thought was a glaring deficit—his height. This created an uncomfortable feedback loop in conversations. Someone would tell him he was handsome; he would reply, "No, I'm not." The person would plead with him to accept that it was true, and after a few more refusals, the person would end up thinking Danny was greedily seeking to hear the compliment over and over. Danny could have stopped the loop with a "thank you," but his habit of minimizing prevented him from really hearing the compliment, no matter how many times it was repeated.

The primary problem with all these thinking errors is that they shape the reality of the person making them. If you do not take action to change your thinking errors, they can directly lead to feeling distressed. Worse than that, they can lead to bad short- and long-term decisions, relationship and parenting troubles, ill health, and general life dissatisfaction. Thoughts are powerful! Your brain is always listening, even when there's no audience except you.

The good news is that there are ways to avoid the thinking errors that lead to assumptions!

If you catch yourself with an elevated pulse, a constricted chest, or other anxiety-related body discomfort, it is likely you are having a negative thought. I can almost guarantee that this negative thought has an error in it! For that reason, it is critical that you do a forensic analysis of your thinking to identify and weed out your negative thoughts, and then balance the thought by trying to locate the actual evidence to support the faulty thinking to counteract it.

Here's how:

- Begin by identifying the negative situation you're in: *Looking for parking.*
- Next, identify your mood: *Frustrated.*
- Then, ascertain the intensity of your mood on a scale of 1 to 10, with 10 being the most intense your mood has ever been: 7.
- Now, identify the negative thought: *I can never find a parking space when I need one.*
- Identify the thinking error: *Negative forecasting combined with all-or-nothing thinking.*

- Balance the negative thought by looking for evidence: *Have you ever tried to park in this area before? How often have you never found parking?*
- If you rate your mood again, it's likely to be about a 2.

It is important to remember that thinking errors are always related to the negative thoughts and *not* the situation. There are no errors in situations, only in the ways people interpret and think about those situations. Just as a friend of mine from Alaska once said, "There is no such thing as bad weather, just bad clothes."

I know that might seem impossible at times. Clients will ask me, "But what if my partner leaves me...I lose my job...or my child faces challenges in school?" These are empirically sad and difficult situations. Although the mood intensity may be high because of the severity of the event, this does not mean that you have escaped a thinking error or two that may be compounding an already deeply and definitively stressful situation.

Working with thinking errors brings us back to assumptions and preemptive problem-solving, or what I like to call the chess game....

Typically, we engage in assumptions when we are feeling insecure about a recent interaction. Then, we launch into a series of overthinking patterns that are focused on preemptive problem-solving in our attempt to make predictions about potential outcomes. Unfortunately, using this methodology to calm our nerves usually ends up exacerbating them instead. There are several challenges with trying to engage in preemptive problem-solving, just like in a chess game:

- Think about it. We play entire chess games in our minds to create multiple scenarios. This is not only exhausting, but it provokes more anxiety instead of reducing it.
- For these chess games, we're guessing about how a person will respond verbally or actively because we don't actually know.
- These chess games yield solutions to imagined problems that were not based on hard evidence and didn't need to be solved in the first place.
- There is no scientific data or research to support the use of preparatory problem-solving in producing effective solutions.
- This kind of advance problem-solving changes future interactions with the individuals in question. If we assume possible conflicts with someone, it will affect our next interaction with them. That other person may question why our demeanor has changed or why we are acting differently.
- Once we start playing the chess game, it can set off a chain of altered interactions and assumptions.

But there's a solution...a way to break the link between reaction and action: *patience*....

It is critical to develop your frustration tolerance and patience and learn to wait until something tangible happens in a social situation before acting on an inference. This may be hard to do at first, but with practice, you can become increasingly successful at it.

Patience is a trait that almost everyone needs to work on. When we become adept at waiting and having patience—even when it is uncomfortable—we find that we are in a better position to avoid assumptions and steer clear of rushing blindly into a decision. We take the time to pause and weigh the evidence. In a recent national survey by Fifth Third Bank to determine just how patient Americans are, it turned out: *not very*. Roughly 80 percent of respondents rated themselves as "being patient," but 96 percent of Americans admitted that they will knowingly consume extremely hot food or liquid that then burns their mouths; more than half will hang up the phone after being on hold for one minute or less; and 71 percent frequently exceed the legal speed limit in order to get to their destination. Myriad studies show that Americans binge-watch an average of six or even seven TV episodes in a single sitting because they are too impatient to delay gratification. Another study noted that respondents became frustrated after just sixteen seconds of waiting for a web page to load and after twenty-five seconds of sitting at a traffic light, waiting for it to change. All of this goes against a predisposition for weighing the evidence, checking the facts, or testing the source of possibilities.

Here are some suggestions for actively increasing your frustration tolerance and improving your patience.

Try making yourself wait.

Practice *not* responding impulsively. We are used to getting immediate feedback in our techno-savvy conditioning. Force yourself to "wait." I have a friend who sorts her emails into two categories: "Fires to Put Out" and "Things That Won't Burn." If something is urgent, she responds right away, but if it requires some thought, needs an action on her part, or could determine a course of action—like committing to a project or following up— she sets it aside and lets it simmer until she is clear about how to respond.

You can apply this method to all sorts of things: posting on social media, saying yes to a date, or agreeing to do a favor, for example. The more you practice this, the more you'll see that most actions and replies need not be instantaneous. And in the long run, you *save* time because you will not have to undo, redo, apologize, or go into damage-control mode. This will help you become more patient, diminish carelessness and redundancy, and teach you to feel comfortable with the unknown.

Another way to become more patient is to stop and rewire perseverant or persistent thoughts.

To do this, I recommend the rubber-band technique. It is a cognitive-behavioral strategy that enables you to pause a thinking error and balance it. It is called the *rubber-band technique* because, in the most famous version, you literally put a rubber band around your wrist, and when you catch yourself in a habitual thinking error, you snap the rubber band, tell yourself to "stop," and distract yourself with a more pleasant thought or memory. Don't snap it so hard you raise a welt on your wrist. Your brain will experience even a light snap as "punishment" and will associate the punishment with the thinking error being addressed, and thus you will gradually learn not to indulge the thinking error. It seems so low-tech, but my clients use it all the time, and it really works.

If you have time, relax, take a breath, and spend a few minutes meditating.

It turns out that meditation is a great tool for developing patience. If you find yourself overthinking a challenging social situation—do not panic. Use meditation, mindfulness, or distraction techniques to calm your brain. Remind yourself that once you engage in overthinking, you will only create more anxiety, which will move you further away from finding a positive solution to your problem.

A calm body and a chaos-free mind can reduce anxiety and strengthen frustration tolerance. Your meditation does not have to be formal—try taking three conscious and deep breaths before acting on an assumption. Table a decision until you can sit quietly with your thoughts. No matter how you create that peaceful mental space, give yourself permission to actively slow down and examine and weigh the question, choice, or situation with judiciousness and tolerance.

Practice self-talk.

Using self-talk will help you to cope with the unknown. Remember to ask yourself if there is evidence to support your concerns. If not, you must remind yourself to wait for more information.

Reinforce yourself by remembering that you have been resilient and have persevered to overcome challenging and troublesome situations in the past. Try repeating something simple like, "Take your time," or "Do not rush into things," or even something like, "A watched pot never boils."

Take a time-out.

If you notice yourself engaging in mental chess games, remind yourself of the trifecta of problems they cause: mental exhaustion, useless problem-solving, and negative social impact. All three can spur negativity and derail your ability to resolve problems in real time.

When we feel tension in our bodies rising to a level of peak proportion, it is important to take a break before we make a rash decision based on assumptions. Being in touch with and scanning our bodies is a preventative measure that can help with anxieties that produce tension. Remove yourself from your surroundings and give yourself a chance to re-center using relaxation, meditation, and self-talk. Bathrooms can be great for this! At work or at home, they can offer a temporary sanctuary, an opportunity to step away from the drama for a moment, close the door, catch your breath, regroup, and assess. This will enable you to re-enter the situation with a new focus. A calm mind can tolerate frustration more effectively than one fueled by tension and anxiety.

Practice gratitude.

According to David DeSteno, a professor of psychology at Northeastern University, "The human mind has a tendency to value the present more than the future." This tendency is the source of why we get into debt and endanger our lives or those of others through reckless or addictive behavior. DeSteno found that practicing gratitude can increase our self-control. It makes intuitive sense—if we are feeling dissatisfied, we tend to want to change our situation as soon as possible. The subjects in DeSteno's study published in the 2016 journal of *Emotion* who completed tasks were offered two options: a certain amount of cash immediately or a higher amount later on. Those who engaged in gratitude practice were more willing to wait for the larger sum of money. When it comes to avoiding assumptions, remember that they lead you down a path of anticipating future negative consequences that may never happen. Keep yourself in the present by focusing on what you are grateful for right now. Are you thankful for your family, your friends, your job, the weather, a vacation? Keep your body and your mind in the here and now to improve frustration tolerance for the future.

Be aware when you lose patience.

Keep track of how often you lose patience with your coworkers or loved ones. As you increase your tolerance for dealing with the unknowns in your world, you can reduce your overall level of frustration. Self-reinforcement (which we will take a deep dive into later on) will help to develop and improve your capacity for patience. When you have consciously stepped back, weighed the evidence, and avoided an assumption, do something nice for yourself. (Remember that when we *act* by rewarding ourselves, we are reinforcing our self-development and healthy behaviors.)

Whichever method you choose, remember that when it comes to avoiding assumptions, patience is an important coping skill.

Along with cultivating patience, another way to train yourself to stop assuming is to accept *not* knowing....

Patience is a trait very few of us do *not* need to work on. Making assumptions is so very tempting because assuming and then believing your assumption is truth is easier than the alternative. The alternative is accepting the uncomfortable feeling of not knowing where you stand with someone or what the outcome of your relationship with them will be. So many people will choose to rush to a bad outcome instead of waiting—often in discomfort—for the facts of a situation to unfold in their own time. Or they do the opposite: they rush to a *great* outcome that has little basis in reality, rather than living through the period of not knowing. They'll think things like, *I have only known you for two weeks, but I already know we are soulmates, and I want to spend the rest of my life with you.*

We would rather push for our worst- or best-case scenario to come to fruition than to remain in uncertainty, expecting it. You need to teach yourself how to sit without that expectation or any expectation at all. When you feel anxious, just say out loud, "I have absolutely no idea what's coming next. It may be wonderful." Repeat it a few times—and remember that your brain is listening!

Wait for the evidence and do not act until you have it. If the evidence never comes, you do nothing. This will feel extremely uncomfortable at first. But the rewards of staying with this discomfort are life-changing. You will begin to see that your patience is as powerful as your ability to rely on yourself to manage whatever life throws your way. Out of this self-reliance will come self-confidence and self-efficacy. And the discomfort of not knowing will transform into the ease of self-assurance, all contributing to Sustainable Life Satisfaction!

As you learn how to stop assuming, it's helpful to understand why we assume....

The main reason we assume is that we tend to bring our histories with us when we enter into new relationships. For this reason, we may feel like patterns are repeating themselves, and people are looking at or talking to us in ways that parallel how others did in the past. In turn, we may believe this will yield similar outcomes.

However, what we forget is that these are not the same people! They have a different set of experiences and life stories than the people we have dealt with previously. Therefore, we cannot predict how they will think or act. What we *can* predict is whether we are going to continue to behave in the same way in all interactions, regardless of whether we are dealing with completely different individuals. For this reason, we need to really work to view each person's feedback as objectively as possible without filtering information through the subjective lenses of their past or our own. You can do this by focusing on the present, the concrete evidence in each interaction, without infusing the situation with supposition or guesswork. There are several ways you can accomplish this.

To eliminate guesswork...

Start by looking carefully for evidence that the person you are in a relationship with has verbally reported a negative statement to you. Determine whether it is real or a statement you may have assumed; no leaps of judgment allowed! If you can't find any evidence, look deeper into your past patterns or relationships to assess whether you're projecting the experiences from another relationship onto this one.

Then, determine whether a core belief from a past experience in your life is being duplicated and causing problems in your present situation....

If so, try to pinpoint when it started. Ask yourself if you are reenacting that belief in your current relationship. If you are, discuss your issues with the other person. Try to come up with a language to identify when it is happening, so you can stop the old pattern and return to the present.

After you do, pay close attention to negative forecasting and any critical internal monologue you have been engaged in with your partner so that they can be aware.

Who might have spoken to you like that in the past?

The way I advise clients to work with this step will work for you as well: Try tracking and disrupting your assumptions. Make a list of assumptions you have about the people in your life, relationships, work, the future, or even in your past. Document those experiences in a journal or even in the note function on your phone. Ask yourself if there is hard evidence to support each one of them.

Pick two or three assumptions for which the answer is "no." Return to the thought-stopping rubber-band technique and apply the practice. Every time you catch yourself making an assumption that is not supported by concrete evidence, give your rubber band a little snap.

Look for similarities between those situations and the ones you are in now. How often are your present situations occurring versus the ones you are guessing at or expecting might occur? Pay attention to the patterns you see.

The thing is, if you really want to avoid assumptions, it is essential to stay in the present as often as possible. If you drift into your past and are reliving negative experiences, talk about it with your partner, your friend, your boss, or whomever you are in the relationship with. When you are not worried about imagined outcomes or what other people are thinking about you, you will be able to focus on how you feel about yourself. Insecurity will be replaced by feelings of self-confidence, inherent lovability, and an inner foundation of Sustainable Life Satisfaction.

As you get better and better at avoiding assumptions, you'll start to see that...

- Your self-worth will grow because you will not be plagued by misconceptions.
- Your self-confidence will rise when you reroute misdirected thought processes toward more effective, fact-based decision-making.
- Your self-efficacy will grow as you become more patient and less impulsive, avoid making assumptions, and increase trust in yourself.
- Your self-respect will strengthen with more reasoned behaviors, meaningful relationships, and confident choices based on facts and not driven by assumptions.
- Your belief in your inherent lovability will be based on experiences and truths, not fantasies and doubts.

Let's review the action steps that can help you avoid making assumptions.

The Sustainable Life Satisfaction steps are all about taking action. You can avoid making assumptions and acting on them in your relationships with others when you remember to:

- Identify when a situation or reaction to someone is making you feel something uncomfortable or unpleasant—

a mood state like anger, fear, sadness, disgust, or anxious anticipation.

- Ask yourself: Do I genuinely know what this person is thinking?
- Ask yourself: Do I genuinely know what this person is going to do?
- Look for irrefutable evidence, and only proceed with a response when you have it.

Let's return to Taylor's situation and explore how these action steps helped her. While we were working together, she began dating someone new—someone she really liked. Because of her parents' chronic infidelity, she naturally started to feel anxious as their relationship got serious.

Step one was: Taylor's relationship with the new guy was causing her to feel anxious and fearful. In Taylor's case, we then had to go directly to step four: only act when you have concrete evidence. For Taylor, this translated as: do not jump into bed with another guy! Trust that if this relationship does not work out for any reason, you will recover and find someone else worthy of dating, and lining up the backup guy now is, to say the least, putting the cart before the horse.

Circling back to steps two and three: Did Taylor know what her boyfriend was thinking and what he was going to do? Here, she had to manage her anxiety every time he spoke with a female colleague or received a call from someone she did not know.

Then, something funny happened when it came to step four: look for factual evidence. Taylor waited and waited for the factual evidence. Finally, after six months with the new boyfriend, she figured she had better elicit the evidence through direct cross-examination. So, one night over dinner, she said to him, "I need to know if you consider me your girlfriend."

The guy's mouth dropped open. "What?"

She got really nervous, thinking he was offended that she would make this bold assumption about their relationship. To her credit, she let herself be vulnerable and asked for the direct evidence: "Please, just tell me—do you consider me your girlfriend? Do you consider yourself my boyfriend?"

"Uh, well, okay," the man said, "since I see that you're not joking with me, I'll say that yes, I started considering us boyfriend and girlfriend four and a half months ago, when we decided to be exclusive with each other and started spending all our free time together!"

So maybe Taylor was still doing some projecting onto the situation that prevented her from seeing factual evidence when it was staring her in the face. (Plus, there was a thinking error: minimizing.) This goes to show that these steps take repeated practice. It also demonstrates how you can make life-changing strides even if you practice the techniques imperfectly. Taylor may have missed an obvious piece of evidence, but here she was—six months into a relationship with a loving, faithful guy—and she had been able to manage her anxiety well enough that she had not resorted to her usual self-sabotaging tactic of being disloyal to preempt her partner's disloyalty. The action techniques helped her begin rewiring her social learning pathways.

When you are not constantly second-guessing what another person is going to think or do, you'll be able to tune into the core strength within yourself. Your insecurities will gradually fall away and be replaced by an improved self-concept and feelings of confidence. This will lead to increased levels of satisfaction and more meaningful decisions and relationships. As Alan Alda once said in a commencement address at Connecticut College: "Your assumptions are your windows on the world. Scrub them off every once in a while, or the light won't come in."

Plus, as you'll see, the fewer assumptions you make, the better you will be at reducing people-pleasing behavior.

CHAPTER 3

Own Your Truth

Reducing People-Pleasing Behavior

One of my clients worked at his family's accounting firm. Josh had tremendous success from an early age, but he could never quite tell me why he had chosen this career path. He had majored in business in college and earned his CPA degree because that was what his father had done, and Josh believed that following in his father's footsteps would make him happy. Before Josh knew it, accounting was the path he was on. It seemed fine. Plus, Josh was good at it. He was accomplishing things that people with a decade more experience aspired to, and he was earning a good salary.

He was doing all the things that were supposed to make him happy. But he wasn't happy! As a matter of fact, he was miserable. When he came to see me, he was deeply conflicted. Josh kept saying that he should be grateful; after all, he was "making good money," as he put it. He wondered if he should go back to school for an MBA. "Maybe if I get an MBA, I can take a *different* path but keep making money?" Yet he seemed frustrated by the realization that his salary was not bringing him any place remotely near life satisfaction.

Then, the pandemic happened. Josh realized that he could keep working for his dad's firm but decided to do so remotely. He moved out west and started to spend a lot of time outdoors, hiking and just being in nature. The more time he spent there, the clearer it became; he loved his family but hated his job. He came to appreciate that he was more interested in sustainability than estate taxes and thought maybe he could apply his skills to financing in the sustainability sector. At first, this seemed like a great idea, but as he continued to consider it, he began to think this might be a safe choice but not an authentic one. Eventually, Josh reached a point where he decided that he was going to leave finance completely. He dipped into his savings and spent a few weeks backpacking and then did an apprenticeship with a community farm project in downtown Los Angeles.

Josh kept deliberating as he applied the Sustainable Life Satisfaction steps—especially facing fears and avoiding people pleasing. Ultimately, he decided he wanted to go back to school for a degree in climate science and the economics of sustainable agriculture. Once he finishes his degree, he will no longer be bringing in quite as big of a salary, but he already looks better and sounds better, and he says he feels like the new relationships he is developing are genuine. By being true to himself, he's on a path that will take him beyond happiness. Some of the people in his life are struggling with his transformation, and he is getting a little bit of pushback, but the people who loved him before still love him. And although his family might not fully see the value in his new path, they certainly value how happy he is. His life turned around because he owned *his* truth—not his dad's truth, not his friends' truth—and stopped people pleasing.

People-pleasing syndrome is dangerous!

In today's hyper-connected world, we have a growing obsession with, and cultural proclivity for, being liked and needing to please others. In fact, the prevalence of people-pleasing behavioral issues among my clients is rampant and takes many forms.

But what exactly do I mean by *people pleasing*? Some credit family therapist, psychologist, and author Virginia Satir for coining the phrase "people pleaser." In her view, a people pleaser is a *placater*—someone who feels that they have no value except for what they can do or be for another person. A universally accepted definition of a people pleaser is a person who has an emotional need to satisfy others, often at the expense of their own needs or desires. We are all susceptible to getting caught up in the people-pleasing syndrome, no matter our age, gender, race, or socio-economic status—nobody is exempt. Likewise, it does not matter what our position is in a relationship—parent, child, partner, friend, employer, employee, or coworker.

I believe that people seek to please others in their lives for both conscious and unconscious reasons, including conflict avoidance. They people please to secure a feeling of indispensability and therefore security, and to reduce fears of abandonment. Their fears of anger and confrontation force them to use "niceness" and "being agreeable" as a type of self-defense camouflage.

Unfortunately, people pleasing can lead to much deeper compulsive behavioral patterns and complicated mental health issues such as fear of rejection, resentment, frustration, anger, addictions, bullying, and even eating disorders. These patterns clearly defeat all the elements of an empowered life—self-worth, self-confidence, self-efficacy, self-respect, and, of course, a belief in one's inherent lovability—and are essentially the opposite of defiant resilience.

People pleasing not only affects our relationships, but it also has an effect on our physical health. Noted psychologist and author Harriet B. Braiker shined a light on this in her book *The Disease to Please: Curing the People-Pleasing Syndrome*. As she described it, "Repressed negative feelings may emerge in the form of migraine or tension headaches, back pain, stomach pain, high blood pressure, or any of a host of other stress-related symptoms. And, under the surface, resentment and frustration bubble and churn, threatening to erupt in open hostility and uncontrolled anger."

Psychologists Robert F. Kushner and Seung W. Choi conducted a study in 2010 of nearly five hundred thousand male and female subjects ages eighteen to sixty-five years old and determined there was a prevalence of unhealthy eating, exercise, and coping-pattern traits among a large sample of overweight and obese adults who participated in the study. One study of coping styles and eating behaviors found that negative coping styles like people pleasing were directly correlated with being overweight— with 54 percent of women identifying with people-pleasing coping mechanisms and 40.3 percent of men.

People pleasing can have darker repercussions as well. Dr. Gabor Maté suggests in his book *When the Body Says No* that suppressing our feelings—as we do when saying "yes" when in fact we mean "no"—is an indicator of a Type C personality, which is "extremely cooperative, patient, passive, lacking assertiveness and accepting…the type C individual in our view suppresses or represses 'negative' emotions, particularly anger, while struggling to maintain a strong and happy façade."

Although still highly debated and far from conclusive, correlations have been found between Type C personalities and certain cancers, like lung and colon cancer. This *may* be because personality affects the immune system, but it may also be because Type C personalities are less likely to advocate for themselves, such as when it comes to healthcare. Either way, the tendency would appear to have a negative effect on one's health. According to research by behavioral psychologist Lydia Temoshok, PhD, author of *The Type C Connection: The Behavioral Links to Cancer and Your Health*, the main personality factors that play a role in increasing breast cancer risk are the suppression of emotions and a coping style characterized by a tendency to defer one's own needs to the needs of others. Clearly, people pleasing is a behavior that diverts us far from resilience, defiant or otherwise.

To find out if you're a people pleaser, ask yourself...

- Do I offer unsolicited advice?
- Do I change my plans at a detriment to myself to accommodate other people?
- Am I resentful because people do not treat me the way I treat them?
- Do I feel like I am always the one whose needs or concerns are considered last in a plan or a situation?
- Do I feel unseen or invisible?
- Do I make time for myself?

- Do I mindfully raise concerns with people when issues arise?
- Do I drop everything when someone needs me?
- Do I look for validation through social media engagement?
- Do I anticipate what others need and act on those guesses?
- Do I feel underappreciated?
- Do I feel preoccupied with the desire to solve other people's problems?
- Do I micromanage people at work or at home?

If you answered "yes" to two or three of these questions, you are at risk of being a people pleaser and need to practice developing and nurturing your sense of self-worth.

If you answered "yes" to three to five of these questions, you're in the danger zone and should prioritize the tools in this chapter.

If you answered "yes" to five or more of these questions, you have probably already developed a habit of suppressing your needs while anticipating and elevating the needs of others. This process may be occurring so quickly that it is almost unconscious. It will take patience to change these habits, as well as an ability to tolerate the fear that comes with separating your identity into an autonomous self. The good news is that it can be done, but it will take time and small steps. Praise yourself for progress and try not to be put off by how exhausting and challenging the task may be. The closer you get to independence, the more you will realize that your effort is going to pay off in more ways than you ever imagined, and you will be on the path to interdependence.

The opposite of interdependence is codependence, or what I like to call *the people-pleasing epidemic*....

The person who inspired me to recognize what a key role people-pleasing behavior plays in human interaction is actually not a psychologist. An integral member of the recovery community, Melody Beattie is well known for insight into and writings about codependency. When I first read her best-known book *Codependent No More*, I found that so many of the attributes she identified as "codependent" applied to nearly all my clients and, in fact, to just about everyone I knew. Codependency is not exclusive to people who have or are recovering from addictions—almost all of us engage, to some degree, in codependent behavior.

I now ask most of my clients to review the list of codependent behaviors in Beattie's brilliant book and identify which ones apply to them. She breaks them down into twelve categories:

- *Caretaking.* Things like pleasing others instead of oneself and overcommitting.
- *Low Self-Worth.* Such as fearing rejection or rebuffing praise.
- *Repression.* Pushing away thoughts or feelings, being afraid to be oneself.
- *Obsession.* Unable to stop thinking or talking about problems.
- *Controlling.* Afraid to let people be themselves or let events play out.
- *Denial.* Pretending a situation or truth is not what it is.
- *Dependency.* Looking for happiness outside oneself, clinginess.

- *Poor Communication.* Tendency to fail to express or overexpress feelings or not to listen.
- *Weak Boundaries.* Persistently letting others cause harm and then wondering why.
- *Lack of Trust.* No faith in other people, oneself, or one's decisions.
- *Anger.* Afraid of being or making others angry or using anger to deflect connection.
- *Sex Problems.* Using sex to caretake, control, or resolve conflict.

Codependent people also tend to be either hyper-responsible or irresponsible, passive-aggressive, and prone to addictive behaviors or hopelessness.

Nearly every client I have ever treated has come to me with at least one of these behaviors, and most with many of them. What I have realized is that all the items on Beattie's list coalesce into the overarching behavior of people pleasing.

Like codependency, people pleasing can take many forms. There is anticipating others' needs and putting those needs above your own, but there is also a version of this behavior that many people do not *think* of as codependency: foisting your help on others. All of us either know or *are* someone who, for their entire lives, has derived their sense of self worth from the help they provide to others. Typically, such people are not good at gauging whether their help is even wanted. They just dive in and start "helping," often against the wishes of the recipient and to the detriment of their own well-being. And then they get angry when their action is not reciprocated or is not appreciated to the extent to which they feel it deserves to be.

Many of my clients have codependent parents from the baby-boomer generation, especially mothers who were raised to put everyone else's needs ahead of their own but now direct a lot of rage at their adult children because their need for appreciation is unattainable. My clients feel endlessly confused. "I don't understand—I didn't ask my mother to come to my apartment and do my laundry, and now she's so mad at me." *That's* codependence on the mother's part.

Like all forms of people-pleasing behavior, foisting one's help on others arises from the desire to secure indispensability. The thinking error is clear: *I am not worthy of love unless I am constantly doing for others.* Like all thinking errors, ones of codependency prevent the person from seeing the reality of a situation, which in this case is that their help is often not experienced by the recipient as *help* but as imposition or interference. Those parents tend to "rescue" their children from solving their own problems when they anticipate their needs, engaging in a form of people-pleasing behavior that, as you will see, can lead to children who grow up with little confidence in their ability to solve problems. This demonstrates how detrimental people-pleasing behavior can be to its recipient.

I have learned from many, many clients that reducing people-pleasing behavior is essential to healthy, *interdependent* relationships.

Remember, one of the core components of Sustainable Life Satisfaction is a belief in your inherent lovability. If you are acting on the thinking error, *I am not worthy of love unless I am constantly doing for others*, you are delegating the belief in your lovability to another person—that is not interdependence. And if that other person does not reciprocate or appreciate and in fact experiences your "help" as interference, then your plan is not working anyway. A lifetime of people pleasing thus erodes your capacity to believe that you are worthy of love.

Chronic people pleasers do not have autonomy in their relationships. They end up merging or getting enmeshed—delegating their feeling of lovability to another person instead of really feeling it themselves. In a healthy, interdependent relationship, both people have independent, full lives and come together to support each other. In a codependent relationship, the support exists without the independence and therefore functions as a crutch.

When people seek to please others in order to feel loved and worthy, the reinforcement for their self-worth comes from outside of themselves. They jump in to help the other person, and if they do get a smile or a "Thanks so much, honey!" then they receive their hit of the feel-good hormone dopamine, and they are "happy." But this is the kind of short-term fulfilment we are trying to avoid, because it is not sustainable. Reassurance from an external source is, by definition, unreliable. It *cannot* be the basis for your sense of self-worth and your trust in your lovability.

One red flag that someone is a chronic people pleaser is if, when a romantic relationship hits a rough patch, they leap to another relationship. I tell my clients who do this: "Be single for a while. Cultivate your autonomous self. Cultivate your capacity for self-love. Then, when you do meet someone whom you are interested in, you can experience them from a place of calm instead of a place of urgency or panic. You can evaluate them based on who they are, not based on the fearful hunger to be part of an *us*."

A great way to start to recognize and overcome your people-pleasing behaviors is to learn to love your own company.

Stop being afraid to be alone! Here are some ways to do this that I've found especially helpful:

- Practice going to a movie or out to a restaurant by yourself. It may seem hard, but it is not as difficult as you might think. Bring a book or catch up on your email.
- Shop alone and pick out something you like without asking anyone's opinion.
- Make a major decision by yourself. Do this by mapping out the pros and cons, discarding assumptions, and, instead of gathering input from others and questioning your action, examining the decision on your own terms. You could start small by going to a coffee shop and bringing a book or catching up on your email. This will help you think for yourself and form authentic opinions without the influence of others.
- Here's the most important tip: do not break long- or short-term plans you make with yourself. If you do, your brain sends a message that a plan you make with yourself does not hold as much value as a plan you make with someone else. Whether it is going to the gym, applying to graduate school, or buying a new car, defaulting on yourself backhandedly decreases your value.

You must value your own company and trust that people will not abandon you, even if you don't drop everything for them. Believing in your inherent lovability means knowing that people will still be there for you even if you have not made yourself indispensable to them or persisted in frantically searching for ways to please them.

It takes practice, because for so many of us, we feel like no matter how much, it will *never be enough*....

I have a client, Casey, who is in her early fifties. She is the proud single parent of a daughter in college. Casey is a classic people pleaser. She had stepped in and solved her daughter's problems for her whole life. Her daughter would send dozens of texts a day to her mother from college with requests like, "Mom, can you make a haircut appointment for me?"; "Can you make me a gynecologist appointment?"; "My professor was mean to me today—what should I do?"; "Can you renew my gym membership?"

When Casey came to me, she did not see these constant texts and requests as a problem. Instead, they made her feel needed. Each one was a hit of dopamine—the feel-good neurotransmitter—for her. And just as she did with her daughter, she bent over backward to anticipate her friends' needs as well.

The problem for her daughter is obvious: this is a college-age person with zero capacity to meet the basic day-to-day challenges of adult life. But Casey's people pleasing created problems for her as well. She was delegating reassurance about her worth, and she got terribly upset when that reassurance didn't come.

Casey was on social media constantly. If one of her friends used the term "BFF" to describe someone other than Casey, Casey was despondent. If two of her friends went to lunch without her, she felt terrible. She frequently issued instructions to her loved ones about how to make her feel appreciated and loved—her daughter was not to leave the tri-state area for college; her friend was to get her a specific designer's purse for her birthday. A simple "Thanks for dinner; it was delicious!" was not enough—Casey needed a full assessment and compliment for every course, every side dish.

You may think Casey sounds needy and high-maintenance, and to an extent, she is, but what I saw was someone racked by feelings of inadequacy and low self-worth. She ran around trying to do for others in a desperate attempt to justify her value through their need for her, harboring an unrealistic hope that their demonstrations of appreciation would fill her bottomless well of self-criticism and doubt. And, of course, the appreciation always fell short, because Casey was trying to secure her sense of self-worth through validation from external sources. Such an effort is inherently bound to fail.

It's not just overindulgent moms!

People-pleasing behavior can lead to high degrees of anxiety and even panic if the fear of failure feels acute, even if there is little or no evidence to support the fear. Consider Micah, a single dad of an elementary-school-aged child. Micah was in his early forties, high-energy, good at his job, and devoted as a dad despite the naysayers in his life who said he couldn't do it, yet he came to me because life felt overwhelming, and he was often anxious and pessimistic.

Micah arrived at my office one day in a state of distress. That morning, he felt his daughter's teacher was abrupt and callous toward him when she said they needed to schedule a conference to talk about "a situation in the classroom" but would not elaborate. Preoccupied, Micah missed his train and was late for our appointment. As he was telling me all this, he started fidgeting and speaking at a breakneck pace because he was so agitated. He paused only long enough to compose himself as he segued right into strategizing about what to do about the "situation" at his child's school.

One look at him, and I could tell his stress hormone—or cortisol—levels were high. His sympathetic nervous system was activated, and he was in full fight-or-flight mode.

It was a perfect time to discuss mood–event consistency.

Mood–event consistency or mood modulation is connected to the thinking errors I talked about with avoiding assumptions....

Physicians and nurses often ask their patients to rate their physical pain on a scale of one to ten, so they can effectively assess and treat it. For the same reason, I ask my clients to rate the intensity of their moods on a one-to-ten scale. That is the first step in a two-part sequence. The next step—which is equally important—is to use that same one-to-ten scale to rate the severity of the event to which their mood is a response.

An event with a severity rating of 10 would be something catastrophic, like a crippling accident or the death of a loved one. A 9 would be your house burning to the ground or a divorce. An 8 might be having your car stolen. Everyday disagreements with family members, friends, and co-workers typically do not rise above a 3 on the event-severity scale. However, please note that for individuals who have experienced severe traumatic life events, like childhood abuse or other significant trauma, this scale may be more difficult to utilize because of flashbacks or disassociation affecting daily life events.

When I'm working with clients, the process looks something like this:

- I ask my clients to rank the importance of a recent event in their lives, which they often rate at around a 1.5.
- I then ask them to rate the intensity of their *mood response* to that event; it's typically between an 8 and a 10.
- When I point out how this disparity demonstrates a lack of mood modulation and ask where they think their mood intensity *should* have been for an event at a severity level of 1.5, they recognize that a number like 1.5 is more reasonable.
- Next, I encourage them to engage in self-talk like: "Does the severity of this life event warrant this intensity of mood? If not, I'm going to work to use steps to bring the intensity of my mood down."
- Finally, I suggest tools such as balancing thinking errors, the rubber-band technique, and/or distraction—like thinking about vacation or even dinner plans—to produce a more balanced mood response.

It's important to strive for "mood–event consistency" personally and socially, or our mood credibility is undermined both in the perceptions of the people in our lives and for ourselves. To others, someone who reacts with excessive intensity to moderately negative events is considered overly dramatic and may not be taken seriously, like Casey. More importantly, poor event–mood modulation undermines our belief in our own resiliency and agency in the world.

Going back to Micah, it was clear his desire to please his daughter's teacher and show people he could be a good single dad was affecting his mood reactivity. After guiding him through mood modulation, I asked him what the level of his mood intensity was for the teacher situation, and he said an 8. I asked him the severity of the event, and he admitted it was about a 3. From there, we moved on to thinking errors.

"What is the situation that caused you to feel anxious today?"

"My kid's teacher told me there was an issue at school but wouldn't tell me what it was."

"You said your mood was anxious, at an eight, right?"

"Yes."

"What was your negative thought about the situation?"

"That my kid may have done something, and the teacher is judging me and doesn't see me as a good parent."

"What are your thinking errors?"

"Fortune-telling? Magnification?"

"Yes, that's right. And do you have any evidence that there's actually something wrong other than your interpretation of her tone and nonverbal behavior?"

"No."

"Could there be another explanation?"

"Yes, I guess so. She could have been rushing and had somewhere to go to, or just had an upsetting conversation with someone else, or maybe was preoccupied."

"Good. Earlier, you said your mood intensity was at an eight, right? And the event severity at a three?"

"Yes."

"Where would you put the event severity now?"

"At about a two, I guess."

"And how intense would you say your anxiety is now?"

Micah laughed. "I think it's down to like a three."

When he came back the following week, he reported that his daughter's teacher was completely relaxed when he met with her; she just wanted them to be prepared for an addition to the curriculum in the coming weeks. It turned out that any issue Micah had perceived had indeed been fortune-telling and magnification. Any idea Micah had that the teacher was disappointed in his child's behavior or him as a parent was an assumption he made, which was rooted in a legacy of his desire to please people, avoid confrontation, and receive validation from the outside world, either through his child or about his parenting to reinforce his sense of worth. These pop-up moments of anxiety are almost always emblematic of deeper issues.

Remember social learning theory?

It shows us how we come to be people pleasers. Based on social learning theory, as would be expected, people-pleasing patterns like magnifying and acting on false assumptions, as displayed by Micah in the earlier example, typically begin in childhood. As a socially learned behavior, people pleasing arises in families where the implicit or explicit message is to put others before oneself. It is important to point out that this happens *all the time*—even in homes where there is not a lot of volatility or conflict. Sometimes, it occurs as a result of modeling codependent behaviors.

People pleasing can also be a way to manage an unstable, chaotic, or even explosive home life. Sometimes, children become placaters or people pleasers because they are forced to step in for a parent who is addicted, ill, or otherwise not able to fulfill caregiving duties. It can make an out-of-control situation feel manageable or simply be a way to "earn" positive attention from a caregiver. For example, they may receive praise like, "You're so good at getting your dad to calm down." They learn tactics like humor or distraction to diffuse tense situations. "Mommy, could you help me with my homework?"; "Can I tell you a story about something that happened today?"

A child's expertise in managing their family's volatility or even managing moods in a non-volatile home can give them a temporary sense of purpose, value, and self-worth, which can stave off fears of abandonment. So naturally, they will go on to use these same people-pleasing strategies in future relationships, believing that these secure a crucial role in the family or any group. Unfortunately, the opposite is true because these behaviors leave the people pleaser feeling ultimately insecure, vulnerable to rejection, and disposable when their actions are not met with reciprocity or appreciation. They put themselves in a vicious loop where this continuous fear of abandonment causes them to mitigate risk using codependent behaviors by trying to find worth through service to others. By doing so, they do not learn to believe in their inherent value. They do not learn to trust that people will stand by them when they are not providing a service. Until they stop leveraging attention, assistance, or affirmation in exchange for securing emotional safety, they won't learn that they are inherently lovable, whether they are attending to the needs of others or not. They will not learn to believe that their intrinsic value is what will foster and secure a relationship in which they are neither dismissed nor deserted.

This makes me think of my client Georgia, who told me that when she was a girl, whenever she brought home one of the paintings or artistic creations she had made in art class or at school, her mother would barely glance at it and then put it aside with no comment. In these moments, Georgia told me, "I ceased to exist," and her response was to crumple up the painting and throw it in the garbage.

Kids—particularly those with under-responsive parents—spend an inordinate amount of time and energy trying to read the adults in their lives. This is a learned behavior that I call *over-reading*. Georgia came to see that if she expressed vulnerability and talked about *herself*, she got nothing from her mother. However, if Georgia talked about her *mother*, then she became interested and responsive. In other words, Georgia received positive reinforcement not for being her authentic self but for subordinating herself to her mother's needs. From these oft-repeated interactions, the message Georgia received about how to act was reinforced and embedded: always make it about the other person. That is very disempowering!

You can imagine how Georgia's self-worth, self-respect, and belief in her inherent lovability were affected by these interactions. By internalizing this learned belief about other people via her relationship with her mother, Georgia became a people pleaser. Remember, my definition of people pleasing is subordinating your needs, desires, wishes, and dreams to what others think they should be—or to what you *imagine* others think they should be. Being a people pleaser inhibits defiant resilience because you are always looking outside yourself for validation.

In my sessions with Georgia, we spent a lot of time on reducing people-pleasing behaviors. Because the patterns embedded by her mother had formed her adult sense of self, Georgia allowed the slightest disappointment or rejection to make her give up on a project or abandon an idea, and her damaged self-concept was affecting both her work and her relationships.

People pleasing is an unsustainable coping mechanism that will ultimately be counterproductive. Children who receive implicit or explicit messages to put others before themselves grow up to overextend themselves in every way in an effort to create order, control, security, and a sense of stability. They also struggle with believing they have the right to be respected and are lovable in their own right.

I've found that mindful communication scripts for saying "no" can really help with this struggle....

This is because clients frequently tell me that they are afraid that saying "no" is going to come across as cruel or uncaring. But it absolutely does *not* have to. Assertive, mindful communication is more honest and can be done in a firm yet respectful way. Be clear, be direct, and, if you're doing it face to face, make eye contact and look relaxed. Take ownership of what is 100 percent valid and within your rights by using "I" statements. Try some of these:

- *I would really love to be able to help you, but, unfortunately, I am already committed at that time.*
- *What you are going through sounds so very hard. I love you, and I am here for you.*
- *That activity sounds like a lot of fun. I do not think it is exactly for me, but I would love to do something else with you at another time.*
- *Thank you for offering to include us in your celebration. I really love spending time with family, and as much as I would love to be there, I am struggling because I have work responsibilities.*

- *I would love to come this weekend, but I have been doing a lot of driving lately, and I would prefer to look at a different date.*
- *This is not a good night for me; I am really tired. How about next Friday?*
- *And...thank you for offering to help, but I would rather do this by myself.*

This is the love language of Sustainable Life Satisfaction!

I mentioned earlier that the opposite of people pleasing or codependence is *interdependence*....

Let's go back to that for a moment.

For our purposes, the term *interdependence* is a way of describing a healthy relationship between two people wherein each person is effectively balancing their needs and the needs of the other in meaningful ways. As you will see, the opposite of interdependence is *codependence*.

In healthy and balanced *interdependent* relationships, people give each other room to grow and flourish as individuals. In *codependent* relationships, autonomous growth is experienced as a loss of control, generating an atmosphere of possessiveness and distrust.

Interdependent relationships are characterized by two people who have separate identities, practice self-compassion, and value their differences. *Codependent* relationships, on the other hand, suffer from merged identities. Consequently, there is predictability and security in an interdependent relationship, whereas in a codependent relationship, there is inconsistency and even chaos, because you are either riding an ebullient high or sinking into, or *dreading* sinking into, a self-concept-damaging low.

Interdependent people sympathize and care deeply for each other, but they do not take on the struggles of their "other" as their own. Because *codependent* relationships are ripe with reactivity, each partner absorbs the mood state of the other, reacting to and for them.

Finally, people in *interdependent* relationships have broad support systems—good friendships beyond their parents and partners—but people in *codependent* relationships tend to isolate and may experience jealousy of their parents' or partners' other friendships and relationships.

Remember, a key feature of *interdependent* relationships is communication wherein problems are discussed as they arise, as opposed to *codependent* relationships, where problems are repressed or ignored and, as a result, are frequently intensified and repeated.

Keep interdependence in mind as you start taking steps away from being a people pleaser....

To stop people pleasing, you must learn to look inside yourself for the reinforcement and reassurance about your worth that you have been seeking from others. Our codependence authority, Beattie, notes, "We are not responsible for anyone else's feelings, although we are responsible for choosing to be considerate of other people's feelings. Responsible people choose to do that, at times. However, most codependents choose to overdo that. We need to be considerate of our feelings, too. Our feelings are reactions to life's circumstances. Thus, etiquette requires that when you discuss a feeling with someone, you say, 'I feel such and such when you do such and such because…' not 'You made me feel…'"

I've distilled this understanding down to three basic action steps. They worked for Casey, Micah, and many of my other clients whose codependency made them prone to people-pleasing behavior. Try them and see how you feel.

First and foremost, don't offer! Be vigilant and catch yourself when you are guiding, problem-solving, making suggestions, recommending advice, or doing things for your family and friends unless you are *specifically* asked to do so, as in, "Will you help me with this?" or, "What do you think I should do about that?" Otherwise, simply listen.

This is going to be difficult if you have a habit of making yourself feel comfortable by jumping in with "help" in the form of offering advice or running errands. But it is okay to be compassionate without offering unsolicited advice or assistance. The reason you want to stop this behavior is twofold. First, contributing uninvited help sets you up to feel underappreciated for your efforts or creates an assumption or hope that your behavior might be reciprocated in the future. This can lead to potential disappointment and resentment. Human beings are fickle and can't be relied upon to engage in behaviors just because you feel they should recognize or reciprocate what you did for them.

Another reason you need to stop offering is because when you do—be it unsolicited advice or assistance—you are sending a message to the other person that you do not think they could have come up with this answer or taken that action on their own. That is rarely something you would want to communicate. I'm sure you have been in the position where you've been offered unwanted advice and wondered why the person offering it did not think you were capable of coming to that conclusion all on your own.

The people in our lives tend to be appreciative of listeners, sounding boards, and safe spaces to vent their frustrations, even if they do not state this directly. Even if it feels like you are doing absolutely nothing by not jumping in with advice and actions, you are giving them an opportunity to come up with solutions on their own. Everyone will benefit! Even—or especially—your children. Listen and wait. If they need your help, they will ask. Your encouraging silence will send them a message that you have faith in their ability while still being there for them as a physical or emotional anchor *should they ask for it*. Anything else veers into people-pleasing territory and diverts them from *their* path toward sustainable satisfaction.

Recently, my client Emily tried this strategy. She was originally concerned that her friends would find her uncaring when she said less and listened more. We role-played compassionate comments she could make without offering suggestions or problem-solving. At our follow-up session, she told me that, to her surprise, the day after she had an opportunity to put what we talked about into practice, her friend texted, saying, "Thank you so much for listening to me last night; it was so refreshing."

The second action step is to only do things that are asked of you when you don't already have plans to do something else. This includes not abandoning a plan you have with yourself— you should treat yourself with the respect and consideration you would give another person. It's important to show your brain that you matter as much as your friends and family members.

It's also important in this step to remember that, as a people pleaser, you will be tempted to try to create a hierarchy of plans and deem some more important than others. In order to rescue yourself from this position, where you are likely to always put yourself last and the people you most want to please first, the rule of thumb is to mindfully say "no" if you already have another commitment. (Look back to the suggestions earlier in this chapter on how to say "no.")

Remember that there's no need to legitimize why you're saying "no," no matter how tempted you may be! Once you start explaining and justifying, you demonstrate ambivalence and open the door to negotiation, which is a big challenge for people pleasers. If you've been defending your "no," it also makes the next action step more difficult.

The third action step is to do things for loved ones, but only because you want to, not because you're seeking validation. I recommend utilizing a resentment check or body scan to evaluate how you feel about taking a requested action even if you may never receive anything in return. *Would you still want to do it?* To see how your body reacts to the idea, follow these steps:

- First, ask yourself what would happen if the action you are being asked to take, favor you're about to do, or conversation you are about to have was never reciprocated or appreciated in any way. Would you still be willing to do it?
- *Pause* for a moment as you intentionally and steadily inhale and exhale for two to four cycles of breath.
- *Now*, bring awareness to your body and *investigate*. Do you feel tightness between your shoulders, in your jaw, or behind your eyes? Is it difficult to regulate your breath?

Is there a hollow or uncomfortable feeling in your belly? Are you tensing up in resentment or shrinking in fear of repercussion?

- If you experience any of these things in your body scan, then you should calmly answer, "No." However, if the body scan is neutral and relaxed, and you would truly like to help, no matter the consequence or reward, reply, "Yes."

As you practice saying "no" during those instances where it feels right to decline without apologizing or legitimizing your response, you will condition the people in your life to be unsurprised by this new behavior. You will have the freedom to say "no" solely because you don't want to do something, even if you *don't* have a competing obligation. You can do things for family and friends because *you* want to do them. You can do them because you have the time, and it does not interfere with higher-priority things in your life.

Once you decide to do something for someone else, remember you're taking an action with the knowledge that you may not receive anything in return, now or ever. Instead of devoting yourself to pleasing others, you'll learn to please yourself, and ultimately, you'll find that when you do, the people in your life will respond in a more meaningful—*interdependent* as opposed to *codependent*—way. In the words of RuPaul Charles, "If you can't love yourself, how in the hell are you gonna love somebody else?"

Once you have become aware and begun to limit your people-pleasing behavior, the next step is to put that energy toward pleasing *yourself*. Since you now realize you will not get reinforcement on a regular schedule from others, you need to provide it for yourself. For that reason, it is important to learn to recognize and celebrate your successes. This will be extremely challenging at first because you are used to delegating esteem and worth to others and will likely have difficulty determining a standard for your success. Your rubric should be created by you and not impeded by expectations or "shoulds" from the outside world. Fortified with that, decide if you are being a good friend, daughter, son, partner, or coworker.

To put it another way, notice and appreciate when you are compassionate and kind. Do not look to others for positive feedback. You are the only person who needs to believe in you. If you do not believe in yourself, no matter how much other people praise or thank you, the message will never translate into a belief in your lovability. If the locus of control is on the "other" for the reinforcement of your value, then any feelings of life satisfaction you have will be transient at best. Pay close attention to when you are meeting or exceeding your standards. It will build self-confidence, self-respect, and feelings of effectiveness—all of which will translate into feelings of lovability.

There is one big exception to these three action steps! If a task is part of an "understood" contract, you should honor that by following through and completing it. I am referring to things like agreed-upon family tasks, including bringing in the groceries or unloading the dishwasher, childcare, or paying bills, as well as academic assignments or work obligations. In these cases, if you feel you're being put into a position of being a people pleaser, you should communicate with your partner, roommate, child, teacher, or coworker and rewrite the contract.

On the road to not being a people pleaser, it's important to measure your progress....

One gauge of whether you have followed these steps and successfully incorporated them into your actions is how you feel during and after doing something helpful for someone else. Do you feel resentful? Do you feel underappreciated? Do you feel stuck or fixated until you receive an offer of praise? If any of those ring true, you are not truly following step three.

These three steps are challenging. For example, rescuing your children is *so* enticing. It is difficult to feel like a worthy parent while you are allowing your child to fail at something you know they could succeed at if you stepped in and helped them. But part of a parent's job is letting your kids know that they can cope when they falter and fail.

It has been slow progress for Casey, but she has been working diligently to retrain her brain to focus on her own actions and inherent satisfaction. We worked out a structure for her daughter's texts and taught Casey to create and maintain boundaries. Yes, she still helps her daughter with medical issues and offers advice (when asked) if she is having challenges at school, but her daughter is on her own when it comes to the basic things, like making an appointment for a haircut or renewing her membership at the gym! We also had to manage Casey's anxiety—people pleasing can be addictive to a degree because we learn to rely on those dopamine hits. I gave her tools to work through the challenges, like the rubber-band technique, as well as mindfulness meditation (which I will talk about later on).

Casey has actually booked a trip to travel across the country by herself to see an old friend and has started volunteering at an anonymous hotline for troubled teens; both of these activities are reinforcing actions—ways for her to cultivate satisfaction in personal accomplishments instead of using others' appreciation as a barometer of her own merit. She has also learned to set her phone to silent for twenty minutes a day while she meditates, and she's deleted social media from her telephone entirely—which has immensely helped in lessening her preoccupation with her friends' behavior toward her. In turn, this has reduced her overall anxiety.

Slowly, Casey is creating new neural pathways and rewiring her brain. She is learning that she does not have to constantly do things for others or receive consistent positive feedback from them in order to feel like a worthy person. If you are used to subordinating your needs to those of friends, family, or people at work and/or guessing what others need in an attempt to secure your indispensability, these will be hard habits to break. But when you stop compulsively offering service to other people and see that they will not abandon you because of it, this will enable you to know that your value as a human being is not in your service, but in your inherent lovability.

As we learn to do these things, a useful skill is to remember to stay in your lane!

Take my clients Josh and Rebecca, for example. I had been working with them for a while, helping them to become less codependent and develop interdependence in their relationship. We applied my steps and saw real improvement!

Rebecca described it like this: "I imagine I'm driving on the highway. I'm in my car, and Josh is in the adjacent lane. I picture us each staying in our own lanes and only merging safely into each other's lanes when we're given the signal or invited."

This makes so much sense. If you merge into someone else's lane without signaling, your cars are likely to crash. Being mindful of this will have a huge impact on how frequently there's conflict in a relationship because you're both traveling together on a road of mutual respect toward Sustainable Life Satisfaction.

Josh pointed out that when he would drift into Rebecca's lane, he would often rush to give advice, problem-solve, or try to fix something. She would perceive this as controlling. He now recognizes that he hadn't been giving her the space and permission to come *to* him or trusting that she would tell him what she needed. He also noted that if he remembers to be patient, they'll be able to support each other and share experiences together in a mutually respectful, loving, and compassionate way. All that it requires is that their cars travel in sync, merging in and out of each other's lanes for miles without crashes, conflict, and codependence.

As you get better and better at owning your truth, you'll start to see...

- Your self-worth increases as you come to realize that you no longer need to control people and situations in order to ensure that the people you love are not going to abandon you, and that reinforcement comes from within, not from others.
- Your self-confidence will stop eroding and will begin to grow as you become more secure in your relationships, which will be based on genuine connection as opposed to your level of service.

- Your self-efficacy will increase as codependence diminishes—connecting in an interdependent, as opposed to transactional, way.
- Your self-respect will develop as you come to believe
- that you are likeable and loveable—despite the fact that you are not doing what others might want you to do when that would impede your own self-actualization.
- Your belief in your inherent lovability will become ingrained as you rewire your brain to understand that people are with you because they want to be, even if you are not doing anything special to serve them. And they will still love you, and even if they don't, your own self-love will transcend the potential loss of someone who does not support your journey to be your most authentic self.

Now that you have a better understanding of some people-pleasing behaviors, here are some actions that will help you to change and stop them from occurring:

Practice saying, "No!"
When you practice this, do not legitimize the "No" by adding all the reasons why you are saying "No." That shows ambivalence. Just be firm and kindly say, "No."

Stop offering advice or doing things (unless specifically asked).
This is difficult for people who like to anticipate what other people want or need. Use restraint and wait to be asked. If someone is "downloading" to you—instead of offering advice, try to simply validate their feelings.

Turn to internal reassurance!
Remind yourself about your positive qualities instead of waiting for others to do it. Reflect on your day and give yourself positive feedback.

Stop apologizing.
Work hard to stop saying, "I'm sorry," when it's not warranted. Even though you may mean well, the words ultimately demonstrate a lack of confidence.

Make your own decision and commit to it.
Do not wait to see what someone else or "the group" wants to do. Do not overthink or worry about anyone expressing their dissatisfaction. Respect and honor your own choice.

Do something for yourself.
Instead of waiting or expecting other people to do pleasant things for you, do something nice for yourself.

And remember not to break your own heart!

Avoiding people pleasing is the path to inherent lovability. The only way that we will honestly believe we are worthy of love is to trust that people will stick around even if we are not acting in service to them—that they value us for *who we are*, not what we can do for them. Otherwise, we will always think there are stipulations attached to why people want to be around us, which backhandedly undermines our belief in our worth.

On a personal note, I, too, have fallen into placating behaviors by saying "yes" and doing things that I do not have the time to do. In the aftermath, I harbor feelings of being overwhelmed, overburdened, and even resentful. The body scans and resentment check-ins that I mentioned earlier in this chapter? I do them too. I have to consciously remain committed to managing my behavior just as much as I recommend the same to my clients. If I am about to say "yes" to something that I know will frustrate me in the future, I mindfully and compassionately say "no" instead.

As the writer Anne Lamott, author of *Bird by Bird*, famously shared on social media: "Oh my God, what if you wake up some day, and you're sixty-five, or seventy-five, and you never got your memoir or novel written; or you didn't go swimming in warm pools and oceans all those years because your thighs were jiggly and you had a nice big comfortable tummy; or you were just so strung out on perfectionism and people pleasing that you forgot to have a big juicy creative life, of imagination and radical silliness and staring off into space like when you were a kid? It's going to break your heart. Don't let this happen."

The less we people please, the more defiantly resilient we'll become, and with that, we'll be better able to face our fears.

CHAPTER 4

Navigating Uncertainty and Dread

Facing Our Fears

I often tell my clients that facing fears is the most critical step in the process of achieving sustainable satisfaction and, eventually, beyond that, defiant resilience. This is because at the end of the day, if you do not have the confidence and faith in yourself to face your fears—if you do not disrupt the status quo and become unstuck from destructive thinking and behavior—decision-making does not matter, closing does not matter, and you won't have a whole lot to reinforce.

As you develop Sustainable Life Satisfaction skills, the aim is not to eliminate challenges and problems from your life. First of all, that is just not possible. Second, if you never had any problems or challenges, you would never be able to develop the competency to manage them. It is important to learn to face and embrace your fears, to walk through them. After all, ignoring or avoiding them is not going to make them go away. I am confident that what you will see on the other side of fear is a life of sustainable satisfaction!

This crystallized for me when I noticed that something was really upsetting my son Steven: he was worried about baseball. Baseball was *the* thing to be doing at recess during second grade, and he was not participating. The more days he did not participate, the more anxious he became. *What was going on?* Turns out he was worried that if he swung the bat, he'd miss the ball and be embarrassed in front of his friends—*so* worried that his fear stopped him from even picking up a bat.

At first, I sent him off to school with the same piece of advice I had given him many times before: "Come home and tell me what fears you faced today." But he returned home one afternoon and said that watching the kids play baseball and not participating *was* like looking fear in the eye, and it did not feel good at all.

"Steven, what about finding out what is on *the other side* of your fear?" He wondered what I meant. I told him, "The fear is that you won't hit the ball and will be embarrassed. Seeing what is on the other side of the fear means doing the thing you are afraid of and paying attention to what it feels like. See if it feels as bad as being on the sidelines, too scared to play ball with your friends."

I doubt Steven fully bought into or trusted my idea, but sitting out the game every recess must really have not been fun, so he gave it a shot. The next afternoon, he came home from school elated. He said he had pushed himself to take a turn at bat, telling himself that whatever happened next, at least he would be *on the other side*. He did get a hit but emphasized to me that the hit was not the important part. "Looking at the kids playing had been scary, walking through my fear to pick up the bat even scarier, Mom. But you're right—the other side of fear feels *great*!"

Walking through fear...I loved that!

Steven's other-side-of-fear experience led to another and then another. He was afraid of skateboards, but he pushed through the fear, and they turned out to be fun! He was terrified of thunder and lightning, but one day he decided to go out into our backyard during a summer thunderstorm. It was wet and loud, but nothing bad happened. As he grew up, he often challenged himself to prove that he could walk through the fear.

Now that he is an adult, I am impressed by how easily he takes risks in social, academic, and professional situations. This is not because he is an adrenaline junkie or an arrogant guy—he is sensible and humble—but he has developed the capacity to compartmentalize his ability and keep it separate from his fear. He has not eradicated fear from his life—he has learned how to use the energy of fear to propel him toward his goals. It may sound like an oxymoron, but mastering discomfort and (as I like to say) making fear your sous-chef is a big step toward Sustainable Life Satisfaction.

How can we overcome discomfort?

To support an empowered self-concept and all that goes with it—self-worth, confidence, efficacy, respect, and belief in your inherent lovability—you must commit to being uncomfortable. This commitment requires believing in yourself and digging into feelings of self-confidence and faith in yourself *even when you're feeling fearful*. It is truly the only way you're going to become and keep being defiantly resilient. When you develop this faith in yourself, you will be able to walk through fear effectively, regardless of what life throws at you.

But I need to caution you: *just because rallying your self-confidence is effective, it will not make facing your fears easy.* People do not like to be uncomfortable—given a choice, we'll opt for easy every time. But this is not how we grow or train our brains to make choices that foster consistent patterns of life satisfaction. Think about exercising: when you're training hard, your muscles ache, you get tired; sometimes, you even want to throw up—but it is when you push through the discomfort that you see results. The brain is a muscle too! This means you have to keep working at something—a habit, a new behavior or mindset—if you want it to improve; otherwise, the neural pathway in your brain will not strengthen. And like any muscle, if you stop exercising, the new behavior will stop growing and may even atrophy. This means we fall back into old patterns.

In other words, it is not as if you learn something and then you are fixed—that is not the case at all. If so, we'd all be perfect. Again, like with regular exercise, if you're working out on a regular basis and you stop, you're going to end up pretty much back where you began. Is there some muscle memory? Sure, at first. But it will not last. That is why if you want to rewire your brain by creating, ingraining, and sustaining neural pathways, you have to commit to a new way of living, especially when it comes to facing fear.

The way to do this is to think about the things that scare us....

The good news is that it is possible to learn to rescue *yourself* from fear-inducing situations. Like most people, I had an entirely different plan for what my 2020 would look like. In over twenty-five years of being a therapist, I cannot recall a time when

I have witnessed such an unparalleled escalation in fears; the coronavirus pandemic and how it disrupted and wreaked havoc on the world—the many lives lost, an unstable economy, unemployment, family stressors, and an unprecedented rise in mental health issues, all amid what is being viewed as a transformative era in governments in the United States and the world—it was overwhelming. But I emphasize to my clients that fear is not something to run from but rather something to welcome and, as I learned from Steven, walk through.

For most of us, fear increases feelings of dread, despair, and anxiety; it can fuel paralysis in our daily lives. The Chapman University Survey of American Fears gathers data on the worries, concerns, and fears of Americans; the personal, behavioral, and attitudinal characteristics related to those fears; and how those fears are associated with other attitudes and behaviors. The survey then ranks the data into Americans' ninety-five greatest fears. The top ten are:

1. Corrupt government officials
2. Pollution of oceans, rivers, and lakes
3. People we love becoming seriously ill
4. Pollution of drinking water
5. People we love dying
6. Air pollution
7. Cyberterrorism
8. Extinction of plant and animal species
9. Global warming and climate change
10. Not having enough money for the future

The list goes on to include relatively common fears, like losing a job or getting a divorce, as well as phobias like clowns and zombies. The bottom line is we spend a lot of time being afraid! And that is *normal*. The key here is not the fear; it is how we *respond* to it. As Nelson Mandela famously said, "The brave man is not he who does not feel afraid, but he who conquers that fear."

There are no quick-fix solutions to mitigate or rid ourselves of all our fears. It takes attention and practice. Our best option is to face and walk through those fears by engaging in tasks to improve our self-confidence and feelings of effectiveness and efficacy in the world. This will lead to active coping.

I suggest actively committing to facing one fear each day. It doesn't matter how big or how small, but doing something— *anything*—out of your comfort zone to disrupt your homeostasis builds adaptability, resilience, and confidence in your effectiveness in the world. It can be as small as making a phone call to someone you're avoiding or filling out an annoying form. It can be a larger task like applying for a job or asking someone out on a date. By facing fears and recognizing that you are resilient in a situation of discomfort or when challenged by an unknown outcome, you will ultimately have a brighter and more hopeful outlook on the future.

To help you make progress in developing and relying upon your self-confidence, I have identified four key areas of our everyday lives where we can diminish and sometimes eradicate fear: work, family, personal life, and the unknown.

Please remember that these methods are most effective when you use them consistently and before your level of fear spirals out of control. In other words, as best you can, put them into action before or when you are just beginning to feel discomfort or anxiety—not when you're in a full-blown panic.

Let's start with our work fears....

It is important to have a sense of agency or control with the goals you aspire to accomplish in your work relationships and environment. Review your goals with your manager—or, if you are self-employed, make a list and assess your priorities for your career. Make sure your goals are reasonable and executable, and consider factors like your training or your abilities, the current economic climate, and the market for your skills. Be transparent about any competing family or other personal obligations and how they may affect your progress. Then, review your goals with an eye toward success and collaborate creatively with your manager, team, or clients to redefine or clarify them for yourself by writing a realistic schedule and list. As you do, you will feel more confident and in control, which will not only assuage fears but also foster a degree of mastery.

Next, take a look at relationship and family fears....

Set goals to deal with big issues and outline expectations for smaller ones. Create an open forum where everyone can express their feelings and play a role. If you are a parent, remind children that it is a benevolent but authoritative relationship. For example, families have expectations around time spent together—mealtimes, weekends, holidays. If there are going to be changes to the paradigm, they need to be addressed in mindful and productive ways, demonstrating mutual respect and an expectation of negotiation. The key here is clarity—knowing the plan is so much less frightening than not knowing.

Many people avoid conversations about hard topics with family members, but, instead of calming a situation, this creates conflict. This is because your avoidance may lead others to act impulsively as a result of your decision not to face the conflict-ridden situation at all *or* because the conflict was handled rashly instead of sensitively. In these instances, no attempt has been made in advance to manage the expectations of other family members, which could have served to reduce tension-fueled situations. Conflict avoidance may seem easier in the short term, but it is more damaging in the long run. It undermines self-confidence and self-respect, as well as feelings of self-efficacy, because your ineffective ability to talk directly to your family members allows anticipatory anxiety to build. Transparent communication accomplishes the opposite.

Being in healthy relationships with friends, family members, and significant others requires an ability to set boundaries. Setting boundaries is *hard*. It can produce fears that the other person will have a negative reaction. However, if we don't set boundaries, we reduce our ability to engage in self-care, which includes prioritizing our needs, and in so doing, we invalidate the idea that we have a *right* to take care of ourselves. This ends up undermining our belief in our inherent lovability. Setting healthy boundaries—albeit frightening at first—will build stronger relationships because you will be building a stronger "self."

I think everyone's biggest fear, the most terrifying of all, is the unknown. If we knew what we do not know, then we most probably would not fear it. Think about it: the primary reason that people fear death is because they have no idea what happens next. Particularly during challenging times, you must lean into your indomitable human spirit and the belief in your ability to face and conquer new and changing situations by employing your problem-solving skills. Having conviction will help you to bounce back from adversity and cope with what life brings instead of spending time in a constant state of fear. The stronger your faith in yourself, the more resilient you will become.

It shouldn't come as much of a surprise that there's a connection between social learning and fear....

Like difficulties with decision-making, staying stuck in fear has its roots in childhood programming. It is natural for a parent not to want to see their children anxious or distressed. For this reason, when a child seems uncomfortable, it is not uncommon for a parent to swoop in and rescue their child from a trouble-some situation. We have all seen or experienced it—the parents who step in and negotiate minor social conflicts for their children instead of letting them work it out, or who give in and do the homework for a child who is anxious about grades, or shelter or coddle them because, as parents, *they* have learned to see the world as a dangerous place.

I have seen this play out to the extreme in my work. My psychotherapy practice is based in New York City, and there is a clear demarcation between my clients who were already adults with grown children at the time of the terrorist attacks on the World Trade Center on September 11, 2001, and those who had young children, were not yet of childbearing age, or were still children. People in the latter group struggle much more with avoiding fear. For so many of them, 9/11 marked the moment when the world became a frightening, irrational place—and these parents began to try to mitigate their fear by taking too much control over their children's lives once they had children. I imagine that, to some degree, the children growing up during the spread of the coronavirus will have a similar experience to those who were young in the 9/11 era.

The concern and resultant behavior come from a good place, but they have grossly undermined the ability of so many younger people to function in the world. Parents leap in when life gets challenging, and now their children do not know how to handle challenges for themselves. They have had far less practice facing their fears because their parents continually rescue them from discomfort. The problem is that when we do not allow children to make mistakes *and* learn to survive them, they do not trust themselves. Across ages, across demographics, 85 percent of my clients battle with this.

However, it is not just those of us who have lived through a terrorist attack, pandemic, or trauma at a level that makes international headlines—everyone has fears, yet the ability to find the agency to face them, and the coping skills to get to the other side, are key to Sustainable Life Satisfaction.

In *Too Much of a Good Thing: Raising Children of Character in an Indulgent Age*, Dan Kindlon writes: "Our children are lucky that they mean so much to us and that we have so much to give. But it is important to be able to distinguish between when we're parenting them and when we're reparenting ourselves as children. Unless we raise them with the help of an inner parent who knows when to say no and be unyielding, our children will never develop the core of strength, independence, and fortitude they will need to be happy. They will, in short, lack character; that unshakeable sense of self that sees us through life's vicissitudes and is the foundation of all our meaningful relationships."

This makes me think of my client, Tara. Her father started a business and, when he retired, handed it off to Tara. But then the father second-guessed every business decision Tara tried to make. "Don't buy from that vendor—that's a terrible idea!"; "You're going to try to expand into *that* market? Why on earth would you do that?" Tara had endured this kind of disbelief in her intelligence and abilities for her entire life, not just in business but in every interaction—like learning to ski, applying to college, parenting choices, and buying a home. Consequently, she became paralyzed, not only in business but in relationships too—as a mother and partner, she had entirely lost her self-efficacy and self-respect.

Tara absorbed a distorted self-concept from her father and believed she was a person who was too inept or unworldly, maybe even too stupid, to accomplish her goals. Her shattered sense of self eventually prevented her from even *trying* to have the kind of life she wanted. For that reason, learning to face her fears was one of the techniques Tara needed to develop to construct a belief in her effectiveness, self-respect, and inherent lovability as building blocks for a satisfying life.

Part of the trick to this is finding the sweet spot between confidence and competence and making fear a friend....

One of the things I tell my clients about facing fears is that we should all try to live life right on the edge of our fear, on the precipice—not *within* or submerged by it—but honestly as close as you can possibly get without falling over the cliff into panic and the abyss. It may sound like an oxymoron, but by embracing your fear, you will find your level of competency. However, once you become homeostatic or comfortable in that new achieve-ment, you will likely also become complacent. So, at that point, it's important to locate the precipice of your fear *again*, set new goals, and embrace new fears. Find the next challenge, and when you do, you'll renew your belief in your competency. This continuing awareness of pushing the boundaries of your comfort zone will build confidence, self-efficacy, and self-respect.

The line between fear and competence will continue to shift, and it is this continually reinforcing confidence that will allow you to keep returning to that space while the line keeps moving!

This is a concept that bears repeating: *fear is your friend*, your sous-chef, your copilot—*embrace it!*

When we do not challenge ourselves, we grow passive, and this leads to a lack of confidence. This is why people who get to the place where they can retire—whether they retire at forty-five or seventy-five—so often fall into a state of despair, depression, or unhappiness. One of the reasons this happens is because they are no longer challenging themselves and consequently feel like they have lost a sense of competency and purpose in their lives. This leads to a lack of confidence and diminished self-compas-sion. However, if those same people take up a task that is mentally challenging—enrolling in a class, mastering a new skill, or doing volunteer work—their competency rises, because now they are learning something that they did not know before; they are walking the edge and developing new neural pathways because with each new task comes a little bit of fear of the unknown, of the new. (You see, fear truly *is* your friend.)

It is important, though, once we have walked through a fear, that we move forward to the next challenge. Anytime we get into a homeostatic experience—anytime we're stuck in the status quo—we run the risk of no longer being in touch with how competent and capable we are as human beings. When we have lost this competency, our confidence is going to start to deteriorate. When that happens, we become more insecure and have less faith in our sense of effectiveness in the world, which can lead to a downward spiral and the very opposite of satisfaction.

Because of this, it's important to understand that confidence is the opposite of fear....

Some might say that courage is the opposite of fear, but I would argue that it is confidence. Confidence is defined as a consciousness of one's powers and abilities—it is knowing that you possess agency. Confidence is not passive. Whereas courage allows us to look at our fears, confidence allows us to walk through them even when we're scared. Once you develop a more confident outlook, you will be able to assess problems more organically and proactively—to walk toward and through fear. If you are not sure that you qualify as a confident person, ask yourself:

- Do you walk through fear, trusting in your ability to reach the other side? Or do you dodge or deny it?
- When you face adversity, do you instinctively become a problem-solver?
- Are you able to turn dreams into concrete goals and proactively *execute* them?
- Are you grateful for what you have but nonetheless continue to strive to improve yourself?
- Are you open-minded, an information seeker, unthreatened by innovative ideas or other people's opinions?

- Even when situations do not work out optimally, do you remain optimistic and believe that experiencing failure can provide valuable information from which you can learn?
- Are you able to live in the moment while keeping an eye on your "edge" and moving with it?

You may feel that you do not possess these characteristics. Or maybe you have grasped a few. But you can still be effective in limiting your response to fear if you are able to manage your daily expectations. It is a daunting task that requires mental diligence and the ability to avoid making assumptions based on negative biases and dire predictions. As we develop confidence, we become better able to walk through our fears.

To find our path through fear, we need to begin by being aware of its power over us....

Have you ever been to the hospital or the doctor and been asked to rate your pain on a scale of one to ten? There is a similar scoring system that we use in cognitive-behavioral therapy: it is called the Subjective Units of Distress Scale, or SUDS. The SUDS score rates emotional pain from one to one hundred. As with the mood-modulation scale discussed earlier, many people rate all their emotions in the range of eighty to one hundred, but your goal as you work with the tools for facing fear is to assess which fears are at a manageable level to face. Which ones can you realistically face?

To do this, list the top five things you avoid out of fear and rank from one to one hundred. As you continue working with this chapter, apply the techniques you learn to one fear at a time. Nobody can overcome all their fears at once!

When it comes to coping with fears at the edge of the precipice, I've found some things that really work!

You can regularly incorporate the following suggestions into your thoughts and daily routine to help you remain optimistic, stay in the present, have confidence in your abilities, and continue to be grounded in an awareness of how often things go right (*not* wrong). This will help mitigate some of the fearfulness.

First, stop trying to be a fortune-teller!

Stay in the present and focus on what is happening in the present so that you can face your fears and not focus on your faulty predictions or the negative outcomes of the past. My clients have found that this on-the-spot technique has actively rewired their brains and helped them redirect their thoughts away from useless, debilitating fears. Remind yourself: "Just because I think it doesn't make it so."

Second, mindfulness techniques can ground you in your body.

Sit in a chair with your feet planted firmly on the floor, your back straight, and your hands on each thigh.

Say to yourself:

My name is... as you inhale; exhale.

Today's date is... Inhale; exhale.

I am currently located at... Inhale; exhale.

Repeat this process three to five times. After doing so, notice if you feel more grounded in your body. If not, repeat the process.

Third, mindfulness techniques can orient you in space and time.

I adapted a practice taught by Jon Kabat-Zinn, who introduced Mindfulness-Based Stress Reduction to the world in the early 1990s.

When you feel fear arising, try this:

- Look around the space you are in. It might be an office, car, playground, dining room, or wherever.
- Now, pick five objects. Say the name of each object out loud. So it might be: *apple, book, computer, coffee cup, eyeglasses.*
- Repeat this circuit three to five times, repeating the name of each object slowly, intentionally, while being mindful of your breathing.
- Do a body scan and see if you feel like you are more grounded in space, more present in the present. Does your brain feel foggy? Is your heart racing? Are you feeling overwhelmed?
- If the answer to any of these questions is "yes," repeat the process a couple more times until you are connected to the here and now—no longer anxious about the future or fretful about the past.

Sometimes, I add a rubber band to this technique and suggest clients snap a rubber band as they state each object. You can try it both ways and see what works better for you.

Lastly, I've found that staying connected to supportive family and friends can really help you cope.

The things we fear will eventually subside, and this process can go more smoothly if we have reliable support. This could be friends or family, a therapist, or a coach—anyone who can help us with a reality check, remind us of past and potential positive future outcomes, and constructively talk us through the "worst case" step by step in order to pinpoint and challenge the validity of fears that become overwhelming. Remember: most human connection fosters confidence and defeats fear.

Whether it be self-care or mindfulness that you're utilizing to combat fear, remember that these techniques are more than memes, so dedicate time to incorporating them into your daily routine. We have probably all heard the truism of putting your own oxygen mask on first. Please do not forget the importance of devoting some of your mental energy to yourself. Practice self-compassion and give yourself the permission to set aside and spend time on yourself, whether it is engaging in some form of exercise, meditating, or just taking some quiet time to be alone. Remember, it is okay, necessary, and effective to put yourself first sometimes. It is always easier to deal with fear (or closing or decision-making) when we're coming from a place of strength and not stress, doubt, or vulnerability.

Of all the ways to work with fear, positive self-talk might be one of the best....

I once helped a client named Ray who, following his brother's death, sold the family business he had worked in for twenty years. Even though he had achieved everything our culture tells us should generate happiness—his finances, marriage, and family life were all in a good place—he was neither satisfied nor happy. Even worse, he was ashamed of not being happy. Turns out he grew up in a social learning environment that was damaging to his self-concept, which is why he suffered from imposter syndrome.

After working together for several months, Ray and I made considerable progress. By learning how to follow his goals to completion, Ray built up the self-confidence and self-collateral that gave him the faith that he could handle starting a business without his brother—he no longer needed external approval to function. He decided to segue into real estate. If you are going to succeed in real estate, at some point, you probably have to buy property. Despite his progress in other areas, Ray still had a lot of fear around situations that tested his capacity to problem-solve on his own. The parameters overwhelmed him: What is a reasonable amount of money to invest? What are the qualities that would make an investment safe? How much of a return should he expect on his first purchase and over what period of time? Is he capable of running the numbers and making the right judgment? Would he fail? Would he embarrass himself and his family? Left to his own devices, Ray might never have taken any action.

Now, you might say, not being able to complete the steps of buying property is a symptom of not *closing* or not *making decisions*. And you would be right. The problems that the six Sustainable Life Satisfaction steps are designed to solve are often intertwined. *Fear* and *not being able to make decisions* and therefore *not being able to close* are especially related. When someone is paralyzed or hobbled by fear, their decision-making capacity is going to be detrimentally affected as well, and they consequently will not be able to execute tasks to achieve their goals.

I worked with Ray on his thinking errors—all-or-none thinking, like, *I cannot do this!*—and mood–event consistency because even when he was just browsing a real estate website looking for property, his anxiety reached a five on the mood-intensity scale. We also addressed action solutions. Because thinking about buying property made him panic, we broke down the problem into small, clearly defined steps, each of which induced a fear he could learn to manage.

One step was to determine how much money he would spend on the purchase. The next fear-inducing step was to determine a viable location. Next was researching what size property he could buy in his chosen location for the dollar amount he had decided on, then the number of tenants, which led to the type and scope of renovation he would need to budget for. Finally, he gave himself a reasonable, achievable timeframe in which to execute these steps.

To quell his fear, Ray used self-talk like the following about buying property: *All I am doing right now is deciding on the amount I can spend; there is no law saying that if you decide on an amount, you have to buy a building…. All I am doing now is scouting commercial properties; there is no law that says you have to buy every available building you drive by in your car….* And so on.

Faced with, "I have to buy a building, or I am a nobody" (all-or-none thinking), Ray folded. But with confident optimism that a positive outcome is possible and the tools to cope—like remaining calm and identifying the problem and the creative solution—when faced with smaller tasks, such as, "I can start by determining a reasonable and safe amount to invest," Ray was able to reach the other side of fear and become both more satisfied and, beyond that, more defiantly resilient.

Self-talk works because your brain hears everything....

As you saw with Ray, self-talk can be hugely helpful for facing fears. When you find yourself wanting to avoid an action out of fear, try repeating one of these statements until you feel capable:

- I am in charge of my fear; it is not in charge of me.
- I am going to channel the energy I get from fear into positive action.
- Fear is my co-captain, my copilot, my sous-chef—it can help me get to where I need to be.
- Conquering fear makes me feel powerful.
- The more I challenge myself to face my fear, the more confident I feel.
- I am not going to diminish my belief in myself by avoiding things anymore.
- I am stronger and more powerful than I think I am.
- Fear does not equal danger; it is more about me than the situation.

As you become more adept at facing your fear, you'll begin to see...

- Your self-worth will develop as you move forward with closing plans, making decisions, and taking action instead of avoiding it.

- Your self-confidence will expand as you live in a mindset of hope and possibility instead of dread and uncertainty.
- Your self-efficacy will become solidified because the act of coping instead of dodging, especially when repeated, will rewire your brain to move into situations with confidence and a plan instead of worrying about them.
- Your self-respect will come from a life of action, not from habitual avoidance.
- Your belief in your inherent lovability will increase as you live in the present—neither fearing the past will repeat itself nor forecasting a future you cannot possibly know.

Part of embodying this self-concept is learning to make fear your sous-chef....

Just in case it is not already clear, I am not only the creator of the Sustainable Life Satisfaction techniques, but I am also an end user. I employ all six of the techniques to meet the challenges of my own life, to take me beyond happiness to defiant resilience. This does not mean I have no fears—it means I have the tools to manage my fears when they arise.

I have developed a personal practice around facing my fears. I start every morning by asking, "What fear am I going to face today?" When I started doing this, I would give myself assignments, like driving places without the GPS, relying solely on my own intuitive navigation system, or starting conversations with strangers, and one time, I managed to slide down a particularly daunting waterslide in an amusement park!

You can do this too. Try lying in bed for an extra minute before getting up and mentally scrolling through your schedule to identify and *decide* how you may be able to face a fear that day, and then *close*. I suggest starting with simple fears, like making a telephone call you have been putting off for a long time, going somewhere new, or simply saying "yes" to an activity or social engagement you would normally avoid. Over time, you will be amazed at how much more confident you feel. Self-confidence, remember, is one of the core elements of a life of self-empowerment.

Again, I have used the words *decide* and *close* to describe facing your fear and seeing what is on the other side. As you develop skill and confidence in any one of these areas, it will make your work in each of the other areas that much easier. The more habitual this becomes, the more you will feel like you can conquer any challenge that life puts in front of you.

If your fearfulness about facing challenges grew out of your childhood social learning, the action techniques will help you create new social learning pathways. Each time you believe you can successfully overcome a challenge, you are retraining your brain to believe, *Yes, I can problem-solve; I can cope; I can achieve much more than I have been giving myself credit for.* In other words, through action, you are developing a sustainable capacity for self-efficacy and self-respect. As Michelle Obama put it during an interview on NBC News, "You can't make decisions based on fear and the possibility of what might happen."

So let's start making some decisions!

CHAPTER 5

We Are All Just Making Our Best Guess

Decision-Making

Sustainable Life Satisfaction is neither static nor stagnant—it is about synthesizing, understanding, and action. We cannot become closers without being willing and able to make decisions, even if that means sometimes making mistakes. After all, most of us make, on average, thirty-five thousand decisions—from the trivial to the monumental—each day! And just to give you a sense of scope, over two hundred of those are about food—*every single day*. It is important to learn to trust ourselves and to have an empowered self-concept and the agency to move forward in life to thrive. And that means making decisions.

Take Suri, for example. As with so many of my clients, it was difficult to the point of being impossible for Suri to take decisive action. When I started working with her, she was in her mid-thirties, yet her response to almost any question I asked was a childish, "I don't know." She was attractive but often had a deer-in-the-headlights expression. Choices both large and small frequently overwhelmed and sometimes paralyzed her, whether it was what outfit to wear in the morning, which meal to order at a restaurant, or much larger decisions—like whether to go back to graduate school and switch careers.

In the ten years since she had earned her master's degree in management, Suri had held the same job as a French teacher at a highly regarded prep school. She had a codependent relationship with her department head, in which he made a lot of the decisions she should have been making for herself. For Suri, the situation embodied the opposite of self-efficacy. She also coached the school's swim team but said the teens did not respect her. She was half-heartedly looking for another teaching job, but what she really wanted was to become a physical therapist, a career that would have made a lot of sense for her because she was athletic and interested in healing and empowering other athletes. However, she believed that her friends in academia and her status-focused family would not find physical therapy a respectable career path. They'd ask questions like, "Why not do something meaningful, like get a PhD in anatomy and become a college professor, or something in sports medicine instead?" And Suri had internalized their disrespect.

Suri is not alone. I have clients in their twenties who stand frozen in the drugstore because they cannot decide which nail polish color to buy and are genuinely concerned there will be familial or social consequences for picking the wrong color. As a result, they frequently "opinion shop" among friends for a consensus. A friend of mine who is an executive at a media company told me he often overhears his young adult interns in the company cafeteria line phoning their parents to ask what they should have for lunch—*tuna salad or cottage cheese?* And it does not stop as we grow older! Some of my older clients come to me because they are miserable in their jobs but cannot decide which path they should take, or perhaps they are financially prepared for retirement but unable to take the next step.

Do you see yourself here to any degree?

Do you find yourself delegating decisions to your partner, friends, family, or even social media? If so, take a moment to consider this: After you have narrowed a decision down to the best possible and most realistic choices, what difference do most decisions *really* make? If you go on a second date, there is no requirement that you go on a third. If you buy the wrong car, you can trade it in. Even tattoos can be removed.

The fact is: most everyday decisions do not really matter that much. It is the same thing with bigger stuff too. If you enroll at a college and are miserable, you can transfer. If you think you will like a job, try it, and if you do not like it, you can take action to change it. Even bad marriages can be dissolved. Few decisions— except for things like having a child—are irrevocable.

I believe that people who suffer over decisions tend to delegate taking action on the decisions they view as significant because they are afraid to commit. A sure sign of delegation is when we begin with phrases like: *All my friends agreed... My parents thought that... My partner is sure that I will...love the job...thrive at the school...be happy in the relationship....*

Because we fear taking personal responsibility for the decisions we make and their potential negative outcomes, we tend to delegate our decision-making. By doing so, we essentially void our ability to take action because it seems daunting, sometimes to such a degree that we stop making decisions altogether. But I promise, you can pretty much always find a door to exit a choice you made if it does not turn out the way you had wished. No single decision is right or wrong because changing course is almost always an option, as long as you have the flexibility of thought and creativity to find an alternative. However, if you do not commit to *something*—if you do not decide—you will never close, and you will never move forward, thrive, or come anywhere near the experience of happiness.

By delegating the responsibility for making decisions, we assign our self-concept to someone else—a person who we feel is more capable. In doing so, we diminish or damage our self-efficacy, which in turn affects our ability to believe in our inherent lovability. We have likely learned this behavior from our role models (probably our parents). Delegating your power leads to dependence (as opposed to interdependence) and an overinflation of others' influence on our lives.

Here's another example. I had a client whose daughter was struggling with writing her college applications. Ruby's mother was so concerned that Ruby needed to follow the right path and go to college that her solution was to write Ruby's applications for her. Although my client thought she was helping her daughter, what she was really doing was sending a clear message that she did not think Ruby could overcome her difficulties by making sound decisions and writing the applications herself. Ruby was accepted into a great college—*the art school of her mother's dreams*—and was miserable. She ended up dropping out and floundering for a couple of years until her mother stopped rescuing her and allowed Ruby to make her own mistakes and develop a sense of self-confidence by doing so. Ruby ended up getting a business degree and is now a day trader who loves the intellectual challenge and unpredictability of her job on

Wall Street. It was a path her mother could not take for her and one that she could also not take for herself until she and her mother developed an interdependent, rather than codependent, relationship.

Making your own decisions will breed trust in your ability to cope with your choices, regardless of the outcome. This newfound capability will develop into pride, which in turn will manifest as feelings of genuine self-worth—and satisfaction will naturally flow from all of that.

But which guess is the best guess?

Guess what? Here is probably the biggest delusion I am going to poke holes through: no one ever actually makes a 100 percent immutable decision—it is not possible. Every decision is ultimately just a guess, some better than others. You will never know unequivocally what nail color choice was best. You will never know if the person you married is the best partner for you out of all the human beings on the planet. Your college experience might be great, but it is possible that another school could have been a better fit. We make a lot of very well-informed guesses, but there is almost never a definitive answer. It was the same with Suri—she could weigh all the factors, but nothing is certain...*ever*.

We might make a guess we have made thousands of times before, but this might be the day it does not play out the way it did in the past. Today, the subway breaks down in the tunnel, and it would have been five times faster to choose to walk to work. Today, choosing that second cup of coffee makes you jittery and gives you a stomachache. Today, your professor snaps at you when you choose to crack a joke to lighten the mood in the morning seminar. Today, you wake up and realize that you are miserable in the job you chose because you believed it was your true calling. Every day, moment by moment, we are *testing* things and hoping for the best possible result.

Remember, if you are someone who is scared of making a mistake and often frozen in life, never moving forward is not an indicator of any sort of satisfaction. Keep in mind that all those people on social media whose lives look perfect are just doing their best...one decision at a time. Your friends were not sure about dipping into their savings for that expensive Caribbean cruise, but they went for it, and look! There they are on Facebook, making memories with their families, like they always do. How can they be so good at life? What they don't post on social media is that the baby cried for six hours every day, and they got in a big fight and did not speak to each other from the Bahamas all the way to Guadeloupe. People tend not to advertise the bad stuff. Other people's "perfect" lives, carefully curated through pictures, only make it seem like their decisions lead to sure things. The picture on social media is a snapshot of a moment in time to which *we* add the movie. It's just that our minds project a very glamorous beginning and end to a film even though the social media snapshot could have been taken during a film noir, not the sweeping blockbuster we create. The person who made the big career change...the friend who finally divorced the husband with whom she no longer had anything in common...the neighbor who moved across the country—they were all winging it too, I promise.

We are all just guessing. Do not accept someone else's guesses. Your parents' and friends' conjectures about your life are filtered through *their* experience about what *seems* best for *them*.

What about you? Other people may have more life experience than you do, but they have their own DNA and their own fingerprint, so their ideas and guesses about life will very likely be different than yours. They may speak with authority about the "right" decisions, but that does not mean they have authority. Only you have the power to make authentic choices for yourself.

Take action!

How do you work with paralysis around making decisions?

Let's go back to avoiding assumptions—when our thoughts do not match up with reality. Remember that Suri did not want to return to school for a degree in physical therapy because she was concerned the people in her life might think that physical therapists had not achieved a high enough level of success, whereas she did not have that concern about being an anatomy professor or practicing sports medicine. Suri was assuming: "If I become a physical therapist, people will think I compromised in life."

Together, we analyzed the factual evidence. How did she *know* people would criticize her path should she choose physical therapy? Had they indicated this to her somehow? Had they criticized other physical therapists? The answer to all her assumptions was "no," and she recognized that she couldn't actually be certain how anyone would feel. Scary, *yes*; based in fact, *no*.

Then, we looked at how much satisfaction she was getting out of the way she was currently living her life. She loved the swim team. There, she felt like she was doing something she was good at, where she felt knowledgeable and successful. So we looked at whether she could move through her fear of other people's reactions to a potential job change by leveraging the authentic satisfaction she found in that single aspect of her job.

The pleasure she found with the swim team led Suri to move toward the decision to apply to graduate school in physical therapy. Of course, that made her very anxious. To help her with this, we broke down what felt like a monumental decision into smaller choices—which tend to come more easily for all of us and which we are more likely to close on.

Suri's hierarchy looked like this:

- Decision 1: Register for, study, and take the GRE.
- Decision 2: Research schools with graduate programs in physical therapy.
- Decision 3: Apply to schools.
- At each step, we agreed that all she was committing to was that *single* step: there is no law saying that if you take the GRE, you have to apply to grad school; there is no law saying that if you visit a graduate program's website, you have to apply to that program; there is no law that says if you apply to a graduate program, you have to accept their offer—why can't you wait and see if you even get accepted first?
- Lo and behold! Suri was accepted to all but one of the programs she applied to. This was such a big boost to her self-confidence that the decision of whether to go back to school was easy, and the remaining one—which offer to accept—was essentially a win-win. In the end, Suri's friends and family surprised her by not being critical of her process and decisions at all! Instead, they were relieved that she was no longer sour and complaining

about how much she hated her job. They praised her for taking action and working toward her own happiness.

Try this for yourself....

Pick a decision, either small or large, and break it down into at least three actionable parts. The bigger the decision, the more actionable parts you will want to find within it. Make the actionable parts as bite-size as is comfortable for you. Remember, there is no right or wrong way to do things. You will find that the incremental pieces are easier to act (or not act) upon, and you will find your path forward.

Remember, each decision is, at best, an educated guess, so keep the stakes in perspective. This also will help you break down tasks and complete them without over-worrying about the consequences of the decision itself.

An easy action to take as you become more adept at making decisions and committing to them is to keep track: write them down. This action becomes a short-term reward and a long-term way to build evidence and reinforce your progress.

And as you examine your decisions, keep in mind how consistent they are with the weight of the event....

In other words, don't take an hour to choose a chef's salad! Decision–event consistency is seeing that you should aim to tailor your decision-making time and energy to the size and complexity of the decision. How much time do you need to read a menu? Probably not more than three minutes; give yourself another two minutes on top of that to decide what to order. When you are shopping for clothes, give yourself ten minutes to decide which pants or sweater to buy. Give yourself three weeks to gather information about what car to lease. Allow yourself three months to research and decide on a new house. Obviously, these are suggested timeframes to give you an idea of how not to belabor a decision. Use them as a guide, not an instruction. The point is to figure out quicker ways to make decisions for yourself as you realize that they're all guesses and that spending too long on them wastes mental resources.

Set reasonable and proportionate time goals for decisions and stick with them. And once you make the decision, no second-guessing! Be a closer, and remember: in most cases, there is no right or wrong answer, but there is a right-enough one. Start with smaller decisions and build up to larger ones. Each decision makes the next one easier.

I ask my clients to rate the importance of their decisions on the same one-to-ten scale we used for mood–event consistency. And again, this is the first step in a two-part sequence. The next step—equally important—is to use that same one-to-ten scale to rate the amount of time spent in making a decision.

If a decision is a three in magnitude but a nine in deciding time, then you know something is off. The weight of your decision is not commensurate with the time you are taking to make it. An event with a magnitude rating of nine would be something big, like ending a relationship or committing to one. An eight might be making a career shift. Daily family and work decisions, like setting up children's bedtimes or buying a new sofa, typically do not rise above a three on the event-magnitude scale.

When you work with this scaled system, you will soon see that seldom do you come up with a better answer after a deep and angsty deliberation than you would have if you went with your intuition, previous knowledge, and experience. When we overthink decisions, we send a message to our brains that it is the undue volume of attention we have given to the proposed action that yielded a potentially positive outcome as opposed to our inherent effectiveness. This backhandedly undermines confidence. By trusting in our decision-making, we reinforce the idea that we can have faith in our capacity to choose—and that it is our natural abilities, not the disproportionate or exorbitant effort, that yielded the result.

Laboring over a decision is not only a waste of time, but also a waste of precious mental energy. People should give themselves just enough time to gather information before making a decision. As we have discussed, the time to deliberate should be dependent upon the weight of the decision being made. Some of my clients are in "C-suite" positions in large corporations, and when they have worked with me in implementing this strategy, they have been able to successfully make major business decisions in just a few hours.

Time is of the essence! Especially *recovery* time....

Recovery time is important in both not rehashing decisions that have already been made and recovering from distressing moods. (Remember how quickly Micah recovered from people pleasing after worrying about why his daughter's teacher wanted to talk to him?) The better you are at controlling your recovery time, the more confident you will feel that you are in charge of regulating your thoughts and moods instead of them regulating you.

I would recommend a recovery time that aims for about twenty minutes for most everyday events. In an ideal world, you might try for ten, but twenty is reasonable. Here's where mood modulation can come in handy. If an event falls between an eight and a ten, you're going to need more time, like for grief or recovering from a traumatic event. But most of life's events are at a three or below, like a spat with your partner, a kid breaking curfew, or a long line at the grocery store when you're running late. These should not consume more than twenty minutes of your life. Maybe even less!

As you learn to balance magnitude and time, you will feel better modulated overall and gain a better perspective on what is really worth getting intensely upset about, and, ultimately, you will feel better. On a couple of occasions, clients have even called me after a breakup or a disappointment at work and said, "Where do you think this falls on the mood–event consistency continuum, and what would be a reasonable recovery time to aim for?"

Remember to keep the importance of your skill at recovering in mind when moving up the hierarchy of making low- to high-stakes decisions. It may not be easy at first, but start by practicing. Make a couple of decisions on your own every day. Start with small decisions, like choosing a restaurant if you're always second-guessing your choices. Then, move on to bigger decision-making, like not asking for advice from a colleague about how to write a proposal at work or not seeking someone else's opinion about whom you should ask out on a date.

Practice mood–event consistency to stop overthinking these decisions once you've made them. Use it if you feel a guess didn't work out exactly in the way you wanted or anticipated. Using mood modulation will help you move through any distressing mood faster. This is important because if course correction is necessary, then so is clear thinking.

Sometimes, I encourage clients to add a rubber band to this process. I suggest they snap when they know their mood is still not consistent with the event or snap to stop overthinking a decision that required a course adjustment. As you use these strategies, you will be surprised by how much more confident and defiantly resilient you feel!

It is important to train yourself to recognize and take the steps involved in decision-making, but it also requires practice....

Try this technique, which I call, "Playing It Through":

- First, name a decision you have to make.
- Now, list the three best options.
- Is there a significant difference between these outcomes? If so, what is it? What does life look like if you don't make this decision? (Here's a hint: as you'll see, sometimes, not making a decision is a decision.)
- Choose one of these options—the three best, or no decision at all. Breathe into any anxiety and trust yourself. Ignore outside pressure.
- After you have made the decision—about a week later for a smaller one and a month or two later for a bigger one—revisit your choice. Are you satisfied with how it worked out? If your answer is yes—bravo! If the answer is

no, that is fine as well—go back to the beginning and assess your other options. Problem-solve how to create a "door" that leads to a close approximation of your next alternative option.

Here and throughout this process, remember achieving the goal of Sustainable Life Satisfaction is never passive! It is important that you not just think about and perform the exercises but *act* on them!

Sometimes, the best decision is to leave the room, so remember, there's always an exit....

Within your belief in your ability to cope and problem-solve is an underlying belief in your competence, and that competence is based on confidence and self-respect. When we feel competent and confident, we feel less like imposters and frauds in our lives, and we naturally feel more loveable. With that comfort comes a trust in our ability to spring back from adversity, and with that foundation in place, it is far easier to make decisions.

Most of my clients come to me with a fundamental disbelief in their capacity to *cope*. People who cope are confident in themselves. They trust that no matter what room they walk into, they will be able to figure out where the exit is. When clients of mine find themselves repeatedly in rooms and situations that do not appear to have an exit, they give up. But I am here to tell you *every room has an exit*. It can be hard to find sometimes, especially if the room looks different from what you expected, but there is a way out; and if there is not one, then you will have to cut a hole in the wall and make one.

My kids have a running joke when they go on vacation with me. Let's say we have booked a whale-watching tour through our hotel, but there was a miscommunication, and just as we are supposed to get into the shuttle to take us to the dock, the concierge informs us that the reservation was never made, and the boat is already full to capacity. One of my kids will inevitably say to the other, "Don't talk to Mom right now! She is in problem-solving mode."

And it is true—I am. It is not that I feel no disappointment and no fear that we won't get to do the one thing that made us take this trip in the first place. It is that I have learned to trust myself to make a decision and produce a solution. Maybe someone will cancel at the last minute, so we jump in the shuttle anyway and take our chances. Maybe there is another whale-watching company with a boat that is not full that morning. Maybe we go on a nature walk today and go whale watching tomorrow. I know from repeated experience that if I stay calm and give myself a moment to problem-solve, a solution will emerge.

The key is giving yourself that *moment*. It is not always easy to find the exit, and sometimes, it looks different than what you expected, but there will always be one. Can you see that in my example, if I gave into the assumption that I wouldn't find an alternative, I'd be giving into an assumption with no evidence?

When I work with a client who insists there's no alternative to a given situation, I ask them how they know that's true. Have they been in that situation before and tried to find an alternative and failed? Or are they assuming, from the outside looking in, that the outcome will be failure? Assuming failure is negative forecasting or fortune-telling. It's just as easy to forecast the positive as the negative. And yet we humans tend toward negative assumptions. Retrain your brain to see the making of assumptions as a gray place, a place where the answer is still unknown. Assumptions should be neither negative nor positive. Unless you have hard evidence, an assumption should not guide your decisions. Assumptions are neutral, and neutral is *not* bad.

When you're trying to problem-solve new decisions for situations that have not gone as planned, it's critical that you keep the negative assumptions and negative forecasting at bay. As you now know, negative forecasting launches your sympathetic nervous system; you go into fight–flight–freeze mode, and you then have less mindshare to devote to creative problem-solving—an impossible situation if you want to set up your brain to best find a door. You never want to take any sort of action from that triggered state. Instead:

- Remain patient and calm.
- Identify the problem and name it.
- Avoid negative assumptions.
- Find, evaluate, and determine alternative solutions.
- Execute a decision.

By engaging in this process, you will find that although it may not be the exact solution you initially started out with, the new action plan you make will likely be close enough to suffice. Can you feel your resilience building? By engaging in this kind of critical thinking, you will develop a newfound belief in your ability to cope and problem-solve in a challenging situation, two important steps in building the confidence for Sustainable Life Satisfaction.

How do we know we're making good decisions?

You may be wondering about this. Since there is no guarantee that we're always making the 100 percent best decision, is there at least a way to learn how to make *good* decisions? Or even *pretty good* ones?

The answer is "yes," but it takes practice. I have been inspired in my own decision-making by a simple but efficient problem-solving model set forth by noted Hungarian mathematician George Pólya in his book *How to Solve It*, which has been a bestseller since 1945. He created a four-step process for problem-solving: *understand the problem*; *devise a plan*; *act on the plan*; and *reflect*. Based on my experiences with my clients, I have added three more steps to the process: *think ahead*; *look for the gray*; and *don't run out of time*.

Start with understanding the problem and coming up with possible solutions.

If necessary, break the problem down into smaller pieces to make each decision less daunting and do research as needed. This strategy will make problem comprehension and options easier and more manageable.

Perhaps it's something like: My lease is expiring, and I have to move. Should I stay in the same neighborhood where the rents are skyrocketing or look elsewhere?

Next, look ahead.

Doing an if…then analysis, or what is a called a "consequent evaluation," of each element of the decision is often helpful in narrowing down your options and naming the pros and cons of each.

So for the previous example, it would be: If I leave my neighborhood, I will be giving up the community I love. If I stay, I will have an increased financial burden.

As you look ahead, watch for the gray areas.

Try to avoid getting stuck in black-or-white thinking and only seeing two discrete alternatives. Engage in creative or out-of-the-box thinking. Brainstorm a little but not for too long (remember to balance decision magnitude and deciding time) as you seek your "gray" solutions.

What if I moved to the neighborhood adjacent to mine, where the rents are still reasonable but where I can still have easy access to my beloved community?

Take the time to devise and map out a plan.

Set deadlines. Allot a few minutes to small decisions, a few hours to mid-size ones, and a proportionate number of days or even weeks to major life decisions. This will help you to close and to believe in your innate ability to problem-solve and take action, ultimately building self-confidence.

Since my lease expires in three months, I can allot myself one month to tour apartments and two months to submit applications, secure an apartment, and sign a lease.

You have a plan—now follow through with it!

Review each of the steps required to conduct your plan to determine whether those steps are realistic and will result in the desired solution.

I can secure a few days off from work to look at apartments and do the paperwork for the application.

Be realistic when you're estimating the time.

If you run out of time, you essentially have refused to decide, which in itself is making a decision. Allowing a choice to be made for you because you abdicated the agency to make the decision for yourself undermines self-confidence and self-respect. (This is the result of inaction—and action is essential.)

If I do not make a decision in a timely manner, I might be stuck in an apartment I can't afford, don't like, or both.

Don't rush to the next decision—review, reflect, and assess.

Examine the solution you landed on and decide whether, in the future, you would arrive at the same solution or possibly consider another one. Figure out if you can use the same method to help solve other problems.

It's important to evaluate your mood state prior to making a decision. Check in with yourself to ensure you're solving for a problem, not for a mood. Mood states can't be solved—they come and go. For example, anger, resentment, or sadness may be uncomfortable, but you can't rush around trying to find a solution to force the mood to pass more quickly. The more fiercely you try to make it pass, the longer it will stay and the more intense it will feel. In fact, when you try to solve for a mood state, you may end up doing or saying something impulsive, whereas when you're solving for an actual problem, you'll be more methodical (hence problem-solving paradigm).

The apartment-deciding process worked so well; I think I will apply the same system to taking a vacation!

I'll say it one more time: it is important to remember that most decisions are best guesses and are fluid, not permanent. They can be changed if the outcome is not as you had anticipated. If you have the mental flexibility to produce an alternative solution, there is a door leading to an approximation of the original choice you made. It may not be the same, but it will likely be something organically similar. Analyze the alternative: this will help to improve the creativity of thought involved in skillful decision-making. Finally, realize that the consequences of giving in to fear and not making decisions are much greater than those of coping with an error in judgment, a shift in plans, a temporary dissatisfaction, a change of course, or opting for that Plan B.

Self-talk isn't just for navigating fear. It's a great tool for decision-making....

Remember what I said about the brain listening?

Here are some self-talk phrases that my clients have found useful as they have learned to become better at making decisions. Try them out and reinforce the ones that resonate for you by, for example, taking a picture of those phrases and making them the wallpaper on your phone, putting a sticky note on your dashboard, or writing them at the top of the page if you keep a journal.

- Statistically, there are a lot more decisions that are neither right *nor* wrong than either right *or* wrong.
- I have the mental flexibility to rewire my patterns and change course.

- I have the ability to create alternatives if options do not seem to be working.
- Making decisions will make me more confident in myself and foster the confidence of others in me.
- Everyone is just guessing most of the time.
- Nobody knows what is right for me better than I do.
- I am the best person to decide my future and my present.
- Choosing one path does not mean the others are gone— we can usually go back and find another way through.
- There are very few irreversible decisions. I repeat: *There are very few irreversible decisions.*

As your ability to trust yourself and make decisions grows, you'll begin to notice:

- Your self-worth will grow as your life becomes more about *action*—about what was done rather than what was left undone.
- Your self-confidence will improve as you cope, problem-solve, and reap the tangible results.
- Your self-efficacy builds because completed actions and their results will send reinforcing messages about your coping skills and form an assuredness in your brain that delegating, wishing, avoiding, or fantasizing never will.
- Your self-respect will increase from feeling like you are achieving a standard of behavior that is commensurate with what you are truly capable of. There are few better feelings than that of a job well done!

- Your belief in your inherent lovability will be fostered as you come to see yourself as a closer who takes thoughtful action and moves forward in life.

Remember to have a plan and stick with it!

Making decisions is the only antidote to decision avoidance. Consistently making smaller and larger decisions develops decision stamina, which increases our level of self-confidence. Doing this also decreases the mental exhaustion that comes with the fear of decision-making. Likewise, actively making decisions will lead you to trust in your ability to cope. Your capacity to cope will translate into feelings of self-confidence and self-worth. These, in turn, will help you build a positive and affirming self-concept. As you become more adept at making decisions, closing will come more naturally, and self-empowerment will develop from those feelings.

As Amelia Earhart says: *"The most difficult thing is the decision to act, the rest is merely tenacity. The fears are paper tigers. You can do anything you decide to do. You can act to change and control your life; and the procedure, the process is its own reward."* And, as you will see, there is a strong connection between making an authentic decision and actually closing it.

CHAPTER 6

Crossing the Finish Line

Closing

Starting is easy, but finishing is hard. This is true for pretty much everyone. Beginnings are exciting—it may be the thrill of a new relationship, launching a project, the first day of school or a vacation, or deciding to have a baby! Things are not as much fun when a relationship hits a rough spot or veers off course entirely, a project gets tedious, exams or coworkers become overwhelming, or parenting becomes difficult.

Over the years, people have asked me what my pet peeves are, and I am honest with them. I have trouble when people do not follow through on their commitments. I admire those who say they are going to do something and then do it. I came up with a term for those people—*closers*—because they finish what they start; they close the deal. If you want a great (and intense) example of what a closer is, watch that iconic scene in the film version of David Mamet's *Glengarry Glen Ross*. Blake, played by Alec Baldwin, motivates his sales team with a vitriolic but spot-on reality check: "A-B-C. A: always, B: be, C: closing. Always Be Closing!"

I have been thinking about the importance of completing things for a long time. At an early age, I became aware that my grandmother completed each task that was given to her. It started in such a small way: whenever I opened a drawer at my grandmother's house—a kitchen drawer to set the table, a desk drawer to find a pencil—they were always orderly and neat. As someone who had a chaotic childhood, like so many of us do, I loved that—the organization, the reliability. There is a relief and ease in having everything where it is meant to be. Of course, this is about more than drawers or organizing your kitchen or office— it is about not leaving loose ends in a project, about honoring a commitment, about not spending your life apologizing, about starting what you finish for your own peace of mind and so that others come to see you and treat you as reliable.

As I grew older, I found myself becoming impatient with the people in my life who did not follow through. I wondered whether they felt that same impatience with themselves as I did with them. I recognized that doing what you say you are going to do is not always easy, for any of us, in every situation. Drawers are one thing—setting up an appointment with a divorce attorney, transferring to a new college, or changing careers is quite another.

I also recognized that finishing tasks brought my grandmother a certain degree of pride, which helped me make the connection between closing and self-concept. I believe that things left undone tend to haunt people and erode their sense of self and functionality in the world as well as their self-worth. If you allow these things to uproot your sense of self-worth and functionality in one area of your life, it does not matter how effective you are in all the other areas. When we do not close, we leave a crack for doubt to creep in, leading to all sorts of unsustainable and unhappy states—from imposter syndrome to distrust in a relationship, from anxiety to depression, from doubt in our inherent lovability to a lack of self-respect.

As someone who works hard to practice what she preaches, I do my best to complete tasks, and I remind myself that I always feel better when I do. When I can rely on myself to follow through on what I have promised myself I am going to do, I feel more confident. I also know that others can rely on me in the same way, which is particularly important in my line of work since people come to me for help with crises involving their emotions, hearts, and lives.

What does closing look like?

Let's take Kali as an example. She was in medical school at the University of Pennsylvania when she first came to see me. She had always thought she would be a doctor, and her parents had encouraged this path—*perhaps a little too much*—but the reality of the training had become overwhelming for her, and she had started self-medicating to get through. More pressure led to more drugs, and by the time she had a full-blown cocaine habit, she knew she needed help.

The first thing I did was convince Kali to take a semester off and go into a substance-abuse treatment program. When she had completed rehab, she moved in with her parents, who had shifted (or perhaps expanded) their expectations for their daughter and were ready and willing to offer support. I suggested that Kali audit some courses at Temple University, where she had done her undergraduate work. She took me up on it and studied things she had never had time for as a science-focused undergraduate, including poetry. She liked it so much that she decided to enroll full time, but not in the sciences—she decided to get an MFA in writing at Temple.

After her first year there, she became involved in the Black Lives Matter movement, which led her to change course again. She told me, "It was the most authentic decision I have ever made, to get out of sciences and into poetry, but now I feel like I want to be a lawyer because I want to practice law to serve underprivileged people and the activists who are fighting for them. I feel like I keep turning to lawyers to help me with my activism, and I want to be one of them."

The last time I met with Kali, she was halfway through her law degree, still sober, and on the road to a life of satisfaction. She worked hard to lean into authentic decisions, but to be able to do this, she first had to ask herself, "Who do I truly want to be?" She actualized this self-concept by combining five desired elements: her self-worth, self-confidence, self-respect, belief in her inherent lovability, and particularly self-efficacy. To break the pattern of a repeated critical inner monologue, Kali applied active self-reinforcement.

Another example of problems with completing tasks is notable with my client Dan, who was struggling in several areas of his life. Dan often told me about his longtime fantasy of buying a broken old classic car to fix up. But he kept putting it off and putting it off. There were several reasons for this. One was that he felt there were other things he needed to close first, like making his quota of client calls at his job, which he struggled with. Another was that his wife worried that tinkering with the engine of a classic car would pull him away from her and the kids on the weekends—another area in which he made unfulfilled commitments. A third was that he was not sure that he would actually be able to get the car to work.

Starting with that third impediment, I asked him, "What is the real goal of getting the car? Is it getting the car to work?" He began to reminisce about working on cars with his dad when he was a kid, and he realized that what he loved best about those memories was not getting the car to work; it was the time spent under the engine with his dad, happily occupied together on a project. So, we clarified that the goal that represented closing for Dan was really just the tinkering.

When it came to the client calls at work, the problem was that when Dan did make the calls and satisfy his quota, he was not self-reinforcing by rewarding himself, so the progress he made in that area did not stick. Dan is not alone among my clients—many make headway with the Sustainable Life Satisfaction techniques, neglect to self-reinforce, and have to start over again. We came up with a two-in-one plan: Dan bought a car that needed *a lot* of work; if he made X number of sales calls in a week, he would reward himself with X number of hours working on the car that weekend. Week after week, he met his goals and earned his reward.

As for his wife's fear that the car would pull him away from the family, the opposite happened. He was so energized by the self-confidence and self-respect that came from being a closer—which involved (1) achieving the goal of sustaining his work productivity while (2) using the car as a self-reinforcement tool—that he became a more engaged father to his kids (they helped with the car too, sometimes) and better partner to his wife. And all that time, the car never left Dan's driveway!

Remember that the ultimate goal is not anyone else's idea of what closing should be. *You* get to decide what the goal is. This is a critical piece to assimilate about closing and one that many clients find requires a significant cognitive shift. People are used to assigning the definition of successful endeavors (closing tasks, plans, short-term or long-term projects or goals) to a predetermined set of parameters. For example, some people may see closing as literally surmounting an obstacle—like climbing to the top of Mount Everest!

Pause for a moment and consider that an objective like this may feel legitimately authentic to them as a determiner of closing. However, it also may be that if they dig deep, a goal such as climbing partway to base camp may not actually be a personal standard or goal they would have set for themselves if that parameter had not already been predetermined as the success model by the outside world.

I have another client named Laurie who dreamed her whole life of climbing Mount Everest. As she saved her money, trained, and planned for the adventure of a lifetime, instead of enjoying the process, she struggled mightily with what would define "quitting." This was a challenging question because base camps are predetermined markers on the mountain by which many people evaluate successful climbs—even hiking this far, about seventeen thousand feet up the mountain, is considered an accomplishment. Laurie needed to evaluate what she was trying to learn about herself from the climb and how she could evaluate and apply the physical act of reaching her goal (climbing the mountain) to the internal act of closing.

What were *her* parameters? What would define closing for Laurie? Could she be honest with herself during the climb and know when she had physically and mentally reached her goal? Could she recognize that anything beyond that would be performative, based on someone else's standard of success? How was she going to be able to determine the difference between stopping because she was done and had closed for herself versus quitting because it was hard without relying on a preset goal? How would she know when, during the climb, it might become closing for people-pleasing reasons (what people would say about her) and less authentic?

These are complicated questions that require soul-searching to reveal an authentic understanding of what you are actually trying to achieve by closing. Is it reaching the summit or having the courage to set out on the climb and do your best? And were you to close what you set out to achieve from a personal growth perspective, when you reach Everest's base camp, do you allow yourself to stop at base camp, or do you need to continue to re-achieve that same personal goal for yourself multiple times by reliving the base-camp climb over again and again as you climb higher? And if so, for whom? If asked why you stopped, can you say to someone that you achieved what you had hoped to by arriving at *your* personal marker of closing? That's what happened for Laurie—she bonded with her climbing group, met the personal physical and mental markers she had set for herself, and felt she had "closed" by the time she ascended to base camp. She decided to be honest with her personal goals instead of chasing external standards of success, said her "goodbyes" and "good lucks" to the group, and spent the next two weeks of her vacation trekking in Nepal. Laurie not only closed, but she did it authentically and had the trip of a lifetime!

Some people might have done what Laurie did—successfully reached base camp—but internally may not have achieved what they had hoped to learn about themselves, either because they authentically hadn't closed yet or possibly because they became so overfocused on what other people defined as a successful trip that they lost sight of their own definition of accomplishment. Closing is personal, not performative. Closing is for you, not the outside world. Closing is a standard you set for yourself, and no one but you can be the judge of your success.

There is a reason why closing is so difficult....

Closing is boring!

Of course, that is not the only reason why, and we'll get into some underlying reasons later, but boredom is a big one. However, with the challenge comes a sense of effectiveness and having been able to conquer the mundane aspects—not just the fun stuff. I can tell you that a feeling of self-efficacy develops into self-confidence and self-respect, and it is priceless. Completing tasks requires accountability, work, repetition, and organizational skills. But let's face it, starting tasks is where the excitement is. "We'll meet every other week, and that way, we'll read twenty-six books in a year!" Then, it is 9 p.m. on a Thursday, the kids are finally in bed, and you are exhausted; do you open to page 108 of *A People's History of the United States*, or relax in front of another episode of *The Great British Bake Off*?

The reason people do not close is that it requires sustained effort, discipline, patience with minutiae, tolerance for a certain amount of tedium, and a whole series of moments when you realize you still have a long way to go to achieve your goal. In other words, in starting, people think they have found "happiness"—but it is neither real nor sustainable happiness they are feeling; it is excitement or elation—an emotional "sugar high"—which is transient. The real feast—*satisfaction*—is in closing.

Here are some telltale signs that you are not a closer....

- Look in your email inbox. Do you have to-be-returned emails that are over a month old?
- Has your treadmill become a drying rack for your fine washables?
- Do you have folders of travel brochures filled with places you dream of going and a column in your budget for travel, but you have not been on a vacation with your family in years?
- Do you eat dinner in silence with your partner, unable to begin a conversation about something that has been bothering you?
- Do you fail to follow through? How often do you say things like: "I am going to call you on Wednesday," or, "I'll pick up milk at the grocery store," or, "I will email the doctor for you," but never do them?
- Do you find yourself thinking about how much you regret all the promises you have broken?

- How often have you asked for an extension or to reschedule something like your income taxes, a term paper, a difficult phone conversation, or a doctor's appointment?
- Is your skill set commensurate with your work or extra-curricular activities? Or do you spend your days resenting what you do or fantasizing about your true vocation instead of taking action steps toward it?
- Does it feel like you can never seem to move forward in your life, yet you often complain or lapse into complacency, exhausting your mental resources on mindless activities that could be devoted to taking action?

If you answered yes to any of these questions, it is not entirely your fault. But that doesn't mean you shouldn't act to fix it!

Have you figured out yet if you are a starter but not a closer?

If you haven't, that is okay—a lot of people do not know. Here is why: As children and as adolescents, we are often reinforced by our parents in the development of our creative ideas and our initiative. This reinforcement can make the actual execution of an idea seem unnecessary. For example, a child might announce, "I am going to build robots," or, "I am going to be a ballerina," and the parents excitedly praise the act of having the idea but do not hold the child accountable for follow-through or the realistic steps that are needed between the concept and the actualization.

In the same way, our parents influence our ability to realize project *progress*. Initially, their support serves as encouragement, but when the process becomes too boring or difficult to execute, that very support makes a goal easy to abandon. For example, parents might praise a child for joining a robotics club or taking ballet lessons and also praise them every time they go to class, so the children have received the reward (praise) during the process; as a consequence, the reward for closing (building a robot, dancing in the school recital) is diminished (or possibly unsought) because the child has received too many rewards before they have, in fact, closed.

This plays out into adulthood. One of the most frequent complaints my clients make is that they have trouble getting stuff done. The adrenaline rush we get as adults from dreaming about a project feels great in the same way it did when our parents told us that we could be the best ballet dancer *ever* or that we were certainly NASA bound! We have all felt that experience of sitting around a dinner table with friends scheming about the next billion-dollar idea, right? We have all heard about books like *The Secret* that tell us that if we just believe hard enough, we can manifest our heart's desire. Mostly, the dreaming ends by the time we have finished dinner or before the book is back on the shelf because taking action is so much more difficult than brainstorming or believing. Think about the times you have joined a new gym and let the membership lapse without ever going, or signed up for an online course and gotten too busy to log in. Maybe you promised yourself that you would switch jobs, apply to grad school, or downsize your home, but never did.

And think about this in terms of relationships—how often have you told yourself that you want to spend time with your child on the weekend, but then when Saturday comes, there are too many chores? Or realized you should get out of a marriage that is destroying both you and your partner, but the follow-through, in terms of both logistics and emotional labor, is overwhelming, so you keep putting it off?

The bottom line is when we do not close, our outer lives reflect this—a messy house, late fees on our bills, poor health, incomplete projects of all sorts. But what really makes not closing an obstacle to Sustainable Life Satisfaction is the emotional toll it takes—the impact on our inner lives.

Especially when it comes to guilt and procrastination...

If your thoughts are things like, *I cannot get past the nagging guilt...I am haunted by remorse...I was blinded by dread....* Remember, these are all unnecessary and unproductive states of mind that likely could have been prevented by closing a situation, conversation, or action—completing something instead of staying stuck in the middle of it.

Our brains appreciate completion. Without closure and the reinforcement that comes from it, our self-confidence and feelings of competence suffer. Russian psychologist Bluma Zeigarnik first pointed this out in a study she conducted in 1927. She discovered that people have far greater recall for tasks that were interrupted and unfinished than for ones they were able to complete. Think about this in terms of your daily life: if you have neglected or postponed sending a difficult email, it will stand out in your mind far more powerfully than the accomplishment of the other ten emails that you sent. Zeigarnik's theory was supported by British psychologists Ian A. James and Katherine Kendell in a 1997 article titled "Unfinished Processing in the Emotional Disorders: The Zeigarnik Effect." Their extensive research illustrated and proved that intrusive thoughts about tasks that we have not completed are pervasive in our brains. In other words, *not closing* leads to these intrusive thoughts, which can result in symptoms of anxiety, depression, obsessions, and compulsions, as well as other psychiatric problems.

And yet no matter how unpleasant these intrusive thoughts can be, we still procrastinate, which prevents us from closing. When it comes to my clients, I would say that at least 85 percent suffer from procrastination when they begin working with me.

So, what causes us to put off becoming closers? The answer lies in the obvious and direct connection between procrastination and not closing.

It starts with a fear of failure or judgment from others, which can cause paralysis.

Being afraid to disappoint the people in your life—your family, your friends, your coworkers, or even yourself—with a perceived or anticipated failure or misstep can cause paralysis. Paralysis slows down the process of closing or brings it to a halt, causing us to get stuck. So often, we set goals that we cannot achieve because they are overly ambitious, or we find them tedious, and instead of following through, we abandon them—because even if they are unfinished, at least we have not failed. Yet this lack of completion or closing leads to the insidious suffering pointed out by Zeigarnik.

This is followed by the possibility that the outcome will be a letdown.

For some endeavors, it is difficult to get to the "end" because the journey has been so much fun, so the idea of closing can feel like a letdown. We have all known people who enjoy the "chase" of dating but not the everyday nitty-gritty of long-term relationships. In situations such as these, it can be tempting to slow down or drag out the process as you near the conclusion. To combat this, try to explore ways to enjoy what you have accomplished after something ends. This will both push you to finish and mitigate the potential letdown so you can continue to reap the benefits of the task even after the job is complete. When we get to active self-reinforcement, I will give you lots of techniques, but for now, try to focus on the outcome on the other side of the task—closing, even at the risk of being underwhelmed, is far better than not closing at all.

Facing challenges with planning and prioritizing can also lead to difficulties in finishing.

When you get deeper into a job or project, the tasks can become more arduous and time intensive. Prioritizing and figuring out how to set aside the right amount of time for what needs to be done is essential. It is critical not to allow issues with executive-functioning tasks to slow the process down to a halt because you risk never closing.

Remember to avoid the tendency to lie to yourself or not see t he whole picture.

There are chronic non-closers who engage in a lot of denial or self-deceit about the act of closing. It is not just that they don't follow through—they do not even carry out the new "best" strategy they developed to complete tasks. And even if you challenge them on that, they are unable to see that they are following through on neither the task nor the strategy to complete it.

Not closing and procrastination are two sides of the same coin.

If you are struggling with habitual procrastination and finishing tasks, there are several methods that may help you change for the better:

- Stop focusing on the possibility of failure; instead, center on the positive aspects of each small success.
- Stay with the task (conversation, commitment, plan) at hand, and do not obsess about the future and what may or may not go right or wrong tomorrow, next week, or next year. "Live in the present moment" is a cliché for a reason—it is useful advice because the more you think about the future, the more you risk paralysis.
- Prioritize and divide things into manageable parts. It is easy to stop moving forward toward closing tasks that are too large. In these situations, avoidance is bound to set in. Execute and close each part before moving on to the next. Keep moving ahead slowly and do not allow yourself to succumb to immobilization.
- Be realistic when it comes to planning. Do not make promises you cannot keep, or you will never close.
- Do not be afraid to reach out for help! Becoming a closer does not mean you have to go it alone. However, remember that closing does not mean dumping your tasks or growth on someone else or overusing a resource.
- Most important: Remember that *you* define your closing. If closing means reaching a point of satisfaction, then you are done. No one needs to agree with your definition. Do not allow anyone to dictate what success, failure, or closing should mean to you. However, keep in mind that

self-deceit does not work—as the Zeigarnik effect shows, your brain cannot be fooled so easily.

Take action! *And* practice closing....

When people do not complete each part, you can imagine the negative assumptions or possible concerns about people pleasing that may be overtaking their minds. "I'm not going to do this as well as someone else would"; "I am forty-eight years old, and no one will hire me"; "What if I do this, and people still don't take me seriously?"; "What if they ask me questions that I can't answer?" Beyond having difficulty finishing tasks because of that, there's also the fortune-telling that can get in the way of closing: "I've always been a slob"; "I have had seven gym memberships and never used any of them—why should this time be different?" You can use what you learned about avoiding assumptions and reducing people-pleasing behaviors to help you with closing. It's critical that you use the Sustainable Life Satisfaction techniques in conjunction with each other. The way I encourage clients to do this is by asking yourself:

- What am I trying to close?
- What are the assumptions I'm making?
- What evidence is there to support these assumptions?
- How is people pleasing affecting my ability to close? Think about family, friends, and the community at large.
- What might I be afraid of that's affecting my ability to move forward?
- What decisions need to be made?

- If I broke down the decisions into smaller action steps, would my fear be more manageable?
- Can I close the original action step now or the smaller, more manageable action steps?
- How did I do?
- Should I make any changes?

Here's a way to take action steps to become a closer....

Start by taking out a few sheets of paper or starting several documents on your computer, one for each area of your life in which you need help completing tasks. One could be "home," another "body/health," another "career," and another "relationships." Write down everything you want to do that you are not doing but wish you were. And I mean *everything*, small and large—no cheating here; you would only be cheating yourself.

Also, and this is important: *no judgment!*

Now, you may find it overwhelming to see all the undone stuff in front of you on a list: taxes, bills, wills, healthcare proxies, family photos taking up space on your phone, piles of unsorted papers, those thank-you notes you put off writing—to the bigger, more amorphous stuff, like finding a couples' therapist and convincing your partner to go with you, or applying for some of those jobs you bookmarked on LinkedIn. The scope will be vast, so remind yourself: this is it—the point is that it is all here, now, where you can look at it and tackle it.

Now, make two columns. Call one, "Things I Can Do Quickly," and the other, "Things That Take More Time." Start by knocking out a few of the tasks in the "Quickly" column. Go online and pay some credit card bills. Put a load of sheets in the washing machine and keep going until they are dried, folded, and stacked in the closet. Buy some stamps and write those thank-you notes. I notice in my clients' lives and my own life that those undone tasks that are visible to us when we walk through the front door of our homes, even though they are small, can really eat away at our self-efficacy and erode our self-respect. Knocking a few of those out right away is an effective way to build self-confidence and provide positive reinforcement to fortify yourself. Try to complete all the smaller tasks (those that will take less than an hour) first.

Not only will you feel empowered by crossing those small things off your list, but you also will have simultaneously created more bandwidth by diminishing the Zeigarnik effect, creating more mindshare for the big stuff.

Next, return to the "Takes More Time" list, and break those longer tasks down into smaller, incremental, manageable tasks. Let's say your boss at the nonprofit has told you that you need to raise X number of dollars in donations by the end of the month. Task one: *Write the boilerplate letter you will send out to all donors.* Task two: *Compile your list of recipients for the letter based on who got the letter last year and new contacts you have made since then.* Task three: *Gather up the addresses.* Task four: *Send out the letters.* And so on.

Every time you complete a task, cross it off—which is, of course, also a type of self-reinforcement. Make it your goal to cross off at least one item from each column every day—or, in the "Takes More Time" column, at least one incremental task that will contribute to completing the larger task.

Some of my clients like to set up the lists in different ways. Since there's no right or wrong way to set up the lists, I'm going to give a few more options. You can also make two columns and order them by "Have a Lot of Interest in Completing" and "Have Less Interest in Completing," or "Critical to Complete" and "Less Critical to Complete." Some clients also mix and match. For example, "Takes Less Time" and "Have Less Interest in Completing." Regardless of how you set them up, it's important to make the lists and cross things off daily. It's also critical to break down more challenging tasks into more manageable bites so that they can be completed and reinforced. And don't forget that these lists are dynamic rather than static, so keep adding to them as new things come up.

If you notice that something on the list continues to get overlooked, you should ask yourself if it's on the list because you said "yes" to something you should have said "no" to. Remember that's a people-pleasing behavior. Just ignoring the item is not going to make it disappear. By ignoring it, you're letting yourself down and potentially also the person to whom you said you would complete it. Admit to yourself when you're not going to complete a task, and either return to the person and renegotiate the terms or outsource the task to someone who will complete it. Outsourcing the task is a way to close. For example, I have a lot of clients who put home-improvement tasks on these lists and never cross them off. They are frustrated with themselves for continuing to overlook them, and so are their family members. Were they to close by outsourcing the project to a handyperson, the task could be crossed off a list and would no longer be a source of feelings of inadequacy, frustration, or incompetence. Remember, *how* you close is not as important as *that* you close.

Above all, set yourself up to succeed....

Here are a few ways you can do this.

- Remember, not everything you have ever fantasized about doing should make the list. If you think you should join the PTSA at your kid's school, do a gut check: *Do I want to do this? Do I have the time to do this?* If the answer is "yes," do not spread yourself so thin that you end up shortchanging your kids, your spouse, your colleagues, and yourself just to participate in the bake sale. It is more merciful for all concerned to say "no" when you need to.

- There is a reason why I suggested you break the lists into small and large and then break the "Takes More Time" list into increments. You will be overwhelmed if you focus on everything at once. This will lead to negative forecasting—*I'll never get this done, so why bother?* Stay in the moment and work with one item at a time.

- Make sure the time frame you are giving yourself to complete tasks is realistic—err on the side of giving yourself too much time rather than too little.

- Remember, how you define closing is personal to you. Define it for yourself; don't delegate the benchmark to someone else.

- And this is important: Do not say yes to doing something for someone that you do not want to do. As discussed in the chapter on reducing people-pleasing behaviors, this will not serve you. Also, do not say yes when you know you will not be able to close the thing you are saying yes to. Get comfortable with saying no.

- And sometimes, it is okay to move the goalposts. When life keeps you from closing—a family crisis, a technology glitch, or an illness—own it. Revise the plan, hold yourself accountable, and change deadlines or goals as necessary—and close, close, close!

What happens when you become a closer?

- Your self-worth will grow as your life becomes more about what is being done than what has been left undone.
- Your self-confidence will improve as you cope, problem-solve, and reap the tangible results.
- Your self-efficacy will build because completed actions and their results will send reinforcing messages about your coping skills and develop an assuredness in your brain that wishing, avoiding, or fantasizing never will.
- Your self-respect will increase from feeling like you are achieving a standard of behavior that is commensurate with what you are capable of. There are few better feelings than that of a job well done!
- Your belief in your inherent lovability will grow because you will stop relying on external reinforcement. You will love yourself more because you won't be riddled with guilt, anxiety, or diminished self-compassion, and the people in your life will pick up on this.

One of the key components of the Sustainable Life Satisfaction techniques is *action!* It is essential that you act and don't just *think* about acting. That is what being a closer and living a sustainably satisfied life is all about.

As you do, remember to commit to your word *and* to your life. Maybe we all need to be a little bit more like former professional baseball player Derek Jeter, who said: "The last thing you want to do is finish playing or doing anything and wish you would have worked harder."

Closing is a crucial step toward feeling a sense of effectiveness in the world. It is about committing to keeping your life in order and honoring your word. As you complete more and more tasks, you will find that your self-confidence and self-respect will grow. You will have a renewed belief in your own efficacy. Yes, it requires patience, but it feels so good! The results will be life-changing, and you'll reap the rewards. By achieving Sustainable Life Satisfaction, you are closer to a life of defiant resilience, which is the final goalpost beyond happiness.

CHAPTER 7

Treat Yourself Well

Active Self-Reinforcement

So far, I have discussed how to avoid making assumptions, reduce people-pleasing behaviors, and face your fears; the importance of making decisions; and how to become a closer. The last Sustainable Life Satisfaction step on the path beyond happiness and defiant resilience is self-reinforcement, a critical component that is slightly different from the others. You have probably noticed that the first five techniques all involve making better choices for yourself and taking charge of your life; the ultimate step involves embedding or hardwiring those techniques.

Sustainable Life Satisfaction does not happen overnight. It requires a steady, daily commitment to practicing each of the techniques. As with any skill—playing the violin or basketball, learning to drive or to cook—you will get better at it as you continue to do it, gradually building muscle memory in tandem with rewiring new neural pathways. It takes work, and sustained work of any kind is a challenge. That is why it is so important that whenever you are successful, you *self-reinforce* each accomplishment you have made with any of the first five techniques.

Conventional cognitive-behavioral therapy, or CBT, teaches the importance of self-reinforcement, but this is one of the areas in which I feel it does not go quite far enough. When I was learning about self-reinforcement in my CBT training, I was told to teach my clients to evaluate their own progress. If they believed they had done something worthy of praise, they were to reward themselves by saying, "Good job!"

That does not work for me. Quite simply, telling yourself, "Good job!" is a thinking solution to an action problem. The action problem is how to wake up on yet another day and close, make decisions, face your fears, avoid assumptions, and reduce your people pleasing in a life through which you have habitually *not* been doing those things up until this point. In the same way that a dog trainer needs to give a dog an actual treat or a pat and not a mere "Good job!" in order to train the dog to sit or heel, you need to give yourself a concrete, tangible reward and not just a self-administered "Nice work!" after you finish a project you have been putting off, complete your college applications, speak before a group for the first time, thwart your assumption that a date will go badly, or whatever it is you are trying to accomplish.

Likewise, for the same reason that someone is never going to be satisfied if they delegate the belief in their worth and lovability to other people, you will not reliably get the kind of reinforcement you need if you rely on others to reward you for completing one of the Sustainable Life Satisfaction techniques. It is imperative that you do it for yourself! If you rely on others for reinforcement, you will lose the ability to believe you can accomplish your goals. Then, gradually, you will let go of the goals altogether, leaving you feeling aimless and unproductive. Without a sense of effectiveness in the world, human beings cannot find sustainable contentment. I would conservatively estimate that when they first come to me for psychotherapy or coaching, more than 75 percent of my clients can't effectively self-reinforce and, as a result, suffer from a lack of self-worth, self-approval, and self-confidence. Positive reinforcement works by presenting a motivating/encouraging stimulus to the person after the desired behavior is exhibited, making the behavior more likely to recur in the future. Positive *self*-reinforcement gives you the self-efficacy to be the one who both recognizes your accomplishments and rewards the techniques you wish or need to develop.

Why does self-reinforcement work?

As I mentioned earlier, I worked at a residential facility for adolescents, providing group anger-control treatment. As part of the project, we assigned homework for group members to practice the skills we taught. As motivation to complete the homework, I offered tangible reinforcers. I offered numerous reinforcers I thought adolescent girls might find appealing, like small earrings and lipstick, but all of them were rejected. What the girls really wanted was perfumed bath soap! I was stunned, but I have never forgotten what I learned about the importance of people authentically deciding what reinforcers work best for *them* as motivators. As predicted, the tangible reinforcer (fragrant soap) resulted in a high degree of compliance with homework, thereby solidifying the treatment techniques I was teaching and increasing behavioral generalization outside of the group.

The father of social learning theory, Albert Bandura, wrote extensively about the importance of having tangible reinforcers as "self-motivators" at our disposal, not just as an effective tool for controlling anger. He said, "People get themselves to do things they would otherwise put off or avoid altogether by making tangible rewards dependent upon performance attainments. By making free time, relaxing breaks, recreational activities, and other types of tangible self-reward contingent upon a certain amount of progress in an activity, they mobilize the effort necessary to get things done. People who reward their own attainments usually accomplish more than those who perform the same activities under instruction but without self-incentives, are rewarded noncontingently, or monitor their own behavior and set goals for themselves without rewarding their attainments."

The thing is…the definition of self-reinforcement has been misinterpreted as positive feedback, and it is not the same thing. It is important to take a moment to note the difference between Bandura's intention when he talked about self-reinforcement and how it is often misinterpreted and taught as solely a verbal reinforcement tool. When I was training to become a psychologist and learning to teach self-reinforcement, I was told to teach people to self-evaluate their performances and actions. If these were worthy of praise, they were to praise themselves by repeating a phrase like "Nice work!" or "I knew I could do it!" This verbal encouragement would then serve as a reward—it seems to make sense, right?

Except that it doesn't. I have come to realize that Bandura was the father of social learning theory for a reason. When we want to successfully reinforce an animal—a dog, a parrot, even an elephant—to direct them toward positive behavior, we give them a tangible reward, such as a bone or a treat, *along* with praise. When we want to successfully reinforce a child's positive behavior or new skill, we give them more than just praise—we reward them with a sweet or an outing or an extended bedtime. Even when it comes to people in our adult lives, we offer tangible rewards like an extra tip for thoughtful service in a restaurant or a thank-you note for a special kindness or a bonus at work. And we pair these tangible reinforcers *with* verbal praise—that is where the "Good job!" comes in.

This pairing is crucial and applies to self-reinforcement as well. When it comes to ourselves, I agree with Bandura's theory: self-reinforcement cannot work for people if they only reward themselves verbally, particularly since we are already battling the desire and even compulsion to see feedback provided outside of ourselves as inherently more valuable.

Self- (not external) reinforcement is key....

Finding effective reinforcers for yourself is necessary to break the cycle of finding the outside-reinforcement paradigm more effective than the self-reinforcement paradigm for determining your worth. As a result of our experience of positive external behavior and rewards, we tend to continue to look to others for reinforcement. When that reinforcement is not forthcoming, we become despairing and frustrated, and we feel devalued. That is because the outside world is fickle when it comes to reinforcement and is not a reliable means to receive consistent rewards for many of our positive behaviors. The more reliant we are on this mercurial source of comfort, the more confused we become about our competence, effectiveness, and worth.

I am sure you have been in a situation where you have thought about praising someone for something that they did or said and then realized after they walked away that you forgot to extend the praise. The positive thought that went through your brain never made it past your lips. That happens to us all the time. People eagerly seek this reinforcement that only comes on an intermittent schedule and then feel despair during much of the time in between. That is why it is critical that we take matters into our own hands, evaluate our efforts, and reinforce ourselves as we see reasonable; in doing so, we have eliminated the confounding external variable, which is out of our control, in deciding on our behavior/reinforcement paradigm. We are in charge of whether we *responsibly* reinforce ourselves regularly, intermittently, or not at all.

This is seldom easy! In fact, it can be incredibly difficult for us to internalize and believe positively about ourselves. Likewise, it is also challenging to construct a set of rules by which we offer ourselves tangible reinforcers and consistently apply them. It feels much easier to delegate, to let the other people in our lives decide what the pattern of rules and rewards will be for things like praise-worthy behavior, merit, or lovability—to let others set the bar.

Put simply, it is easier to be told that we are "good" or "did well" (or not) than to determine the inherent goodness of our actions (or not). The good news is that you can shift this tendency! Practice asking yourself if you would reinforce someone else in a similar position, and, if so, to what degree?

Ask yourself things like:

- If my co-worker finished the presentation that I just completed to the same degree of success I had, would I determine their presentation a success? Would I offer to take them out for coffee or a glass of wine to celebrate their accomplishment? If so, celebrate!

- If my partner or spouse completed a project they had been working on for years, would I determine that its completion was a success? Would I suggest that we celebrate? Should I then celebrate my own successes?

- If I saw a family member working hard at making decisions when decision-making is a challenge for them, would I comment and maybe suggest a treat or special event after a certain period of that hard work? How long would I suggest that a family member apply themselves to developing a new skill before suggesting a dinner to celebrate the accomplishment? If the answer is "yes," or "it's time to celebrate," do something nice for yourself. Remember to really think of this as a family member and not yourself—it will be much easier!

Questions like these can guide you. We tend to hold ourselves to impossibly high standards, often far exceeding the ones the people in our lives hold *us* to. Because of this, their action/reinforcement scale is different from yours. You need to learn to be more practical and realistic about the standards by which you gauge yourself, to allow for opportunities for self-reinforcement on a regular schedule based on *those* standards—*your* standards—and not expectations from others.

Separately, if we're receiving feedback from the outside world that we feel we have not earned because the task was actually too easy, or we feel bad about our overall performance in life, that positive feedback from the people in our lives may be desperately sought yet simultaneously dismissed. You have heard the saying, "It goes in one ear and out the other." When we receive external reinforcement—especially if it is solely verbal and not tangible—it does not always last or feel meaningful. I like to tease my clients by telling them that if they hear a particular compliment one million times, it will never be enough, but if the person doing the complimenting brought them a bouquet of flowers or a latte, or gave them an extra week's vacation or extra credit on an exam, they would be more likely to pay attention (as Bandura pointed out), but *still*, they would be unable to assimilate the compliment into the schema they have of their worth!

That is because human beings are not easily fooled by compliments that they feel they do not deserve. These can almost become *unmotivating* because they reinforce feelings of inadequacy, contributing to what you may have heard called "imposter syndrome" or "imposter phenomenon." This term coined by psychologists Pauline Clance and Joe Langford is the "psychological experience of believing one's accomplishments came about not through genuine ability, but as a result of having been lucky, having worked harder than others, or having manipulated other people's impressions," and it affects men and women pretty much equally.

I have found that everybody struggles to some degree with feeling like a fraud or an imposter in their lives. It may be a sense of unworthiness for a promotion, a feeling of inadequacy as a parent, or an all-pervasive sense of "not good enough." This is because very few people feel accomplished and effective in all areas of their lives all the time. And as a result, they feel like a fraud when receiving compliments because they believe they are not fully deserving. For example, you could be having a great month at work, but if you're not closing in other areas of your life—maybe your house is a mess or you were too busy to pay your bills—you might not weigh the praise you have gotten at your job commensurate with your success at work in light of not holding yourself to a certain standard in your home or finances. Thoughts like these cause people to live in a state of perpetual disappointment, which is why, when you are honest with yourself—not acting out of fear, assuming, or people pleasing—you are your own best evaluator and judge of your accomplishments.

Treating yourself well is more difficult than you might think....

Before you say, "I can do that!" I'll be honest with you—self-reinforcement is actually quite difficult. You would think that rewarding yourself for accomplishing your goals would be easy, right?

It isn't.

At this point, you have likely noted a recurring theme: that so much of our learned behavior is introduced and starts during childhood. We are taught to look to the outside world for our reinforcement.

Learned behavior from parents and other adults starts in childhood, where so many of us learn to maneuver for that parental accolade, gold star for conduct from our elementary school teacher, or soccer trophy. As we get older, the rewards shift, and the hunger for them intensifies. Not only is it about achievements—like a dream college or a job title—but we are trained in our culture to seek material rewards, such as a fatter paycheck, a fancier house, a year-end bonus, a car, or a designer bag, as signs of our inherent worth. Because this is the sort of environment we are generally raised in, especially in the United States, I have to repeatedly remind many of my clients to *self*-reinforce, and it takes a while before they can get the hang of it. They will readily do the thinking-solution and mood-modulation steps; they will close a task they have been putting off for weeks; they will face their fears and finally jump off the high dive at the community pool or ask someone on a date, but when I say, "And what reward did you give yourself for that?" they respond, "Oh, I forgot...." The remarkable thing is once they start remembering to self-reinforce, the report I consistently receive from them is how much easier it becomes to sustain the first five active Sustainable Life Satisfaction techniques.

Our human reliance on outside forces for reinforcement is not effective in the Sustainable Life Satisfaction paradigm. It is important to make a cognitive shift from aspiring and needing reinforcement and praise from others to embracing and accepting self-praise. Outside reinforcement is too unreliable when it comes to developing and hardwiring new thoughts and actions. I have challenged clients to self-evaluate and actively reinforce themselves, so they can master their belief in themselves.

When they do, I advise them to make sure they're using real and meaningful rewards....

As B. F. Skinner, noted American psychologist and behaviorist, demonstrated, sustaining the positive-reinforcement loop will help you to continue working harder and more efficiently on a long-term basis, so pick reinforcers that you feel strongly and positively about.

Here are some simple yet reliable examples of tangible reinforcers:

- Give yourself a gift or a treat.
- Take yourself on an outing—this can be a walk around the block or a dream vacation.
- Take a nap or a bubble bath.
- Cook yourself a special meal or make a cup of coffee or tea.
- Buy yourself flowers or a nice bottle of wine.
- Get a pedicure or a shoeshine.
- Engage in a task or activity you enjoy—go for a run, read a new book, or reorganize your spice rack.
- Write an affirmative statement about yourself that reflects your progress or success and, in so doing, own your truth!
- And as we learned from closing, even checking things off on an analog to-do list can be a tangible reinforcement.

You get the picture. Decide what is best for you to actively reinforce and acknowledge your value and the work you are doing to become your best self.

And as you do, here are a few things to remember....

- *Tangible* reinforcement means something real, solid, or substantial. It implies *doing* something, not just thinking about doing it! You need to follow through.
- However, *tangible* does not have to be expensive. I have a friend who rewards herself for completing small tasks during the workday with a five-minute break in her yard and time to putter around in her garden.

- Sometimes, pausing for a moment to write an affirmation in a notebook is a tangible reward because you have given yourself proof of accomplishing a task that you can look back at, doubling the reward! Plus, writing down a success is indelible proof of it and helps create a basis for positive evidence to help combat any challenges in the future.
- Remember that some person's tasks that require rewards will be another's reward—like walking the dog or folding and putting away the laundry.
- Make the reward proportionate to the behavior you are reinforcing. Returning an email you have been putting off might mean stopping work ten minutes early. However, finishing a proposal or presentation you have been working on for months might mean a vacation.
- And do not beat yourself up! Self-reinforcement should be positive, not negative. Skinner found that learning and behavior are strengthened and modified by reinforcement, paving the way for psychologists like Bandura. Skinner saw self-reinforcement as an example of a self-regulatory process in which individuals reward themselves *if* their behavior matches self-prescribed standards of performance and *if* a favorable event (tangible reinforcer) is associated with a behavior—only then will that behavior will be strengthened and more likely to occur in the future.
- Whatever you decide to do, make sure you identify the act of reinforcement as something that you are doing as a reward. Tell yourself you are going for that walk, eating that slice of cake, or buying that book because you have made progress working toward achieving your potential.

As you reward yourself, remember that improving your ability to self-reinforce takes time....

But the rewards are worth the effort, so be patient!

Phillippa Lally, a health psychologist, showed in her study called "How Are Habits Formed: Modeling Habit Formation in the Real World" that becoming habituated to a new behavior pattern takes, on average, sixty-six days (that's two months) but can take as long as eight and a half months, depending on the scope of the behavior and your brain's response to the shift.

Based on further analysis by researchers at Utrecht and Leiden Universities, the average is about three months. They found that: "When striving for long-term goals (e.g., healthy eating, saving money, reducing energy consumption, or maintaining interpersonal relationships), people often get in conflict with their short-term goals (e.g., enjoying tempting snacks, purchasing must-haves, getting warm, or watching YouTube videos). Previous research suggests that people who are successful in controlling their behavior in line with their long-term goals rely on effortless strategies, such as good habits. In the present study, we aimed to track how self-control capacity affects the development of good habits in real life over a period of ninety days. Results indicated that habit formation increased substantially over the course of three months, especially for participants who consistently performed the desired behavior during this time."

Okay...I know most of you looked immediately at the three months and thought, *Three months! That sounds like forever. And eight months? Well...*

You should instead think of this time as an opportunity to be patient with yourself. Learn to relieve yourself of the expectations and pressure that changing your behavior is going to be easy and resolved quickly. Allowing from two to eight months will afford you the opportunity to make mistakes every so often and forgive yourself for them. It is really important to integrate this step—forgive yourself for mistakes, and do not use the mistake as an excuse to abandon everything you have been working toward.

Change takes time, and that time offers you the chance to practice discipline. It enables you to have faith that focusing on you is just as important as anything else in your life. Use the allotted time to set up good habits for your body and mind that will benefit you and serve as reinforcement for a lifetime. The key to this is to set your sights on a clear and specific goal. In other words, instead of deciding, "I am going to change my eating habits and become a healthy person," set a goal like, "I am going to stop eating sugary snacks after dinner." And then consistently reinforce yourself during the process (just not with sugary snacks after dinner!).

When you close and reinforce one goal, immediately set another....

Once each week, state your overall goal—for example, applying to refinance your mortgage, earning a promotion, or overcoming a fear of public speaking. Know that your personal goal is outside of your control because it is affected by the outside world. Then, write what you believe are concrete steps, *within* your control, that will bring you closer to your goal. This could be filling out the paperwork for the bank mortgage refinancing, setting up a study schedule to prepare for the certification course necessary to move to the next level at your job, or perhaps accepting an opportunity to speak in front of a group. You can pick anything—as long as it is not affected by variables in the outside world. It has to be in your control. Then, you can determine your effectiveness at completing the concrete steps. This evaluation has to be done by you and not manufactured by reinforcement or reassurance from the outside world.

Once you have set a goal to reinforce, analyze it regularly within the context of the first five core Sustainable Life Satisfaction techniques.

Ask yourself:

- What decisions did I make that affected my goal?
- Were these decisions I made on my own?
- Have I been honest with myself and avoided assumptions while making the decisions?
- If not, how can I avoid those traps moving forward?
- Was I consciously acting to please myself and nobody else?
- If not, how can I work to focus more on my authentic choices going forward?
- Did I face my fears?
- If so, what were they?
- If I didn't, what tools can I use to face them?
- Did I follow through and "close" on taking action toward my goal? (If you didn't, make sure that the action steps were broken down into small enough chunks to execute successfully.)
- Then, ask: What are the next steps I can take toward achieving my goal?

- How did I feel about myself today?
- After reminding yourself of the long-term reward of closing on your goal and accomplishing something that matters to you, actively self-reinforce in the short term.
- Keep track of your answers in a journal or in the "notes" app on your phone. This is a way to chart your progress and also hold yourself accountable. And, of course, when you feel confident you have accomplished your goal, reinforce yourself accordingly.

And make this your mantra: self-reinforcement is not selfish!

As children, we are often taught that we are selfish if we focus our energy on doing something nice for ourselves instead of for others. What we are not taught is that if we are not able to do wonderful things for ourselves, we will burden someone else with that task. It is important to recognize that you have the same value as anyone to whom you would give tangible rewards. You are giving yourself these rewards when you have decided that you have earned them. If you work for them, then you have to be willing to accept the reinforcement you give yourself. Do not delegate that power to others; learn to own it.

It's not "self"-ish to take care of your *self*. The decreased need for approval from others and the increase in self-reliance to determine the reward for your actions serve to increase self-confidence and decrease feelings of inadequacy. Adding this to your toolkit will help you to maintain your path of Sustainable Life Satisfaction.

Over the years, as I've worked with clients, I've found some great ways to reinforce the qualities we want to develop.

Here are a few of the best ones:

- Write out a list of tangible reinforcers. This will be different for every person. Pick concrete things that you enjoy. Have some free or lower-budget things on the list so you can give yourself daily rewards, even for smaller successes with the techniques. Also have some bigger-ticket items on the list for when you knock out one of those longer-term, multi-part tasks, like finishing a big project or ending a destructive relationship.

- Make sure the list includes things that feel like rewards to *you*. I have a friend who has a specific system of self-reinforcement. When she is working with one of the Sustainable Life Satisfaction techniques—for example, no longer people pleasing by codependently helping her son before he asks for help—she sets a goal: *for the next month, I will not offer until I am asked*. Once the goal is set, she buys herself a present—something she has wanted for a long time. This might be a book or an overpriced but lovely moisturizer. Then, she wraps it in pretty paper, tapes it up, and ties a ribbon on it—the whole deal! She dedicates herself to meeting her goal using the techniques of Sustainable Life Satisfaction, and once she can confidently say to herself that she's met one, she gives herself her present. Of course, you do not have to wrap packages—you might just order something online but not take it out of the mailing envelope until you have solidified the behavior you want to reinforce. And, of course, it does not have to be things—never underestimate the value of a reward like a nap or a nice cup of coffee! Remember, there are no right or wrong ways to self-reinforce. It just needs to be something more tangible than a verbal or nonverbal "nod" to yourself. After that, whatever feels authentic *to* you is the perfect reinforcer *for* you.

- Be truly clear about what task you are going to give yourself a reward for, what comprises completion of that task, and what reward you will give yourself when the task is completed. To make sure that your brain gets the message about what task you are rewarding yourself for completing, try to give yourself the reinforcement as close in time to your completion of the task as possible.

- My client Dan, whom I discussed in the chapter about closing, is a perfect example of someone who figured out how to tailor his self-reinforcement to his unique interests as well as to his own understanding of what a reward was. He loved tinkering with old classic cars, and he also realized that the tinkering itself was the reward, not the getting-the-car-to-work part. He made tinkering with the car his self-reinforcement for calling a specific number of clients at his job. And don't forget: he ended up deciding that tinkering was more important than getting the car to run. His decision about how to self-reinforce also helped him learn something about his personal definition of closing when working on cars. As a result, cars became the ideal self-reinforcement tool for him—but, of course, you need to find the self-reinforcer that works best for you.

Here are some steps that will help improve your ability to actively self-reinforce....

- Start by putting in enough effort to believe that you have earned the rewards you want without turning to another person or the outside world for permission to reward yourself. It is not up to others to determine what reinforcers you have earned or what will motivate you. It is up to you to decide. You are your best and only judge.
- Take responsibility for the follow-through on reinforcing yourself for a job well done. Do not avoid the actual purchase or execution of the reinforcement you have promised yourself. If you decided to reinforce yourself by taking a day off work and going to a basketball game or saving up enough money to go on vacation, buy those tickets or open up that bank account! If you decide to write affirmations, write them.
- Do not cheat! Do not give yourself the reward before you complete the task or action, and do not reward yourself for *almost* getting it done. Remember, it is reinforcement for actions taken, not a participation trophy.
- Do not seek approval or appreciation from the outside world in the form of gifts, bonuses, etc. Seeking feedback is problematic because it is usually inconsistent, sometimes nonexistent, and often misdirected. It can lead to experiencing feelings of resentment, despair, purposelessness, frustration, and anger instead of support and encouragement.
- It is critical to appreciate *yourself* and the work that you do. Choose reinforcers that bring you joy, and remind

yourself that you worked hard to earn them. Try not to people please when choosing a reinforcer and pick something that you think someone else would enjoy doing with you (so that is why you landed on that). Try not to pick something you will feel guilty about later—eating a pint of ice cream if you are on a diet will send a confusing message to your brain—or choose something because you think you should, such as rewarding yourself with a bike ride even though exercise is not your favorite activity.

- Plan your rewards in advance. But as you do, make sure that if you are working toward a long-term goal, like making a career change, you break it up into manageable parts. In this way, you reinforce yourself along the way with small goals that you can easily achieve. For example, start researching the new job you want and make a list of people you want to talk to about the transition. The point is to commit to executing whatever it is that you promise yourself you are going to do.

The more you self-reinforce, the better at it you will become. Not only will you become more sustainably satisfied and defiantly resilient, but also...

- Your self-worth will increase organically as your brain begins to recognize that you think of yourself as loveable.
- Your self-confidence will grow as you meet your goals and accomplish the things that matter to you in life.

- Your self-efficacy will expand, especially because self-reinforcement is so directly connected to achieving goals.
- Your self-respect comes with working the Sustainable Life Satisfaction techniques to completion and acknowledging that you have done so.
- And your belief in your inherent lovability will increase as your need for external awards and approval decreases.

Remember, I've made self-reinforcing the final step in Sustainable Life Satisfaction for a reason!

Well, two reasons, actually....

First, self-reinforcement should accompany each of the other five techniques.

Second, as I said before, and I am repeating because people find it *so* hard to believe, self-reinforcement is the most difficult technique for most of us, even though the only person it involves is *us*. People just have a really challenging time giving themselves tangible rewards for their own achievements.

I have found this in my own life as well. I have become a religious self-reinforcer because the rewards I give myself pave the way for me to practice the Sustainable Life Satisfaction techniques that enable me to achieve a steady state of self-empowerment. Here is a perfect example: As you know by now, I love going to the theater, so one of the rewards I give myself when I complete an SLS task is to buy myself an orchestra seat to a play. Once, when I was at the box office picking up tickets for a Broadway show I was excited to see, the person in the ticket booth looked at my Orchestra Row D seat and said snarkily, "My, you take good care of yourself, don't you?"

"Yes, I do," I replied matter-of-factly to show I felt good about it.

Part of recognizing your self-worth and believing in your inherent lovability—key ingredients in Sustainable Life Satisfaction—is not to delegate rewarding your accomplishments to other people. When we avoid delegation, we become our most fulfilled, adaptive selves. And that is why, as poet and civil rights activist Audre Lorde put it, "Caring for myself is not self-indulgence, it is self-preservation...." Self-reinforcement is last on my list because it cements and habituates the first five techniques and the art of living the life you wish for and that I wish for you!

CHAPTER 8

Contentment in Body, Mind, and Situation

Beyond Happiness

We've come to see that the state of being beyond happiness is where you arrive when you have a well-developed capacity to avoid assumptions, reduce engaging in people pleasing, face your fears, make decisions, and close and when you are able to reward yourself for your own accomplishments. It is when self-worth, self-confidence, self-efficacy, self-respect, and self-love coalesce in you and become second nature. These outcomes do not guarantee that nothing bad will ever happen to you again. Being human means that you will face injury, illness, loss, sorrow, and other forms of upheaval and chaos. Living a life of sustainable satisfaction means you will be equipped with the inner power to face your painful experiences and continue to thrive even when you're not happy. *Beyond happiness* is a state of defiant resilience.

I have told you some stories about my son Steven—how he figured out how to get to the other side of fear and how his childhood illness helped put me on the path of beyond happiness—and now, it's time to share a story of my other hero of defiant resilience, my daughter!

Alexa is and always has been a fighter. Once she sets her sights on something, there is absolutely no stopping her. When she was a junior in high school, I discovered that she had a moderate reading disability that had gone undiagnosed for a long time because her compensatory strategies were so adept that I did not realize that she was facing challenges. It was by the end of her freshman year that I had begun to suspect something was not quite right because she was working for an insane number of hours to get her homework done—no child should have to spend as much time as she did on assignments. Her grades were good but not great for a kid who was putting in the painstaking work she was and in such an organized and responsible way. Why did it seem like she was still struggling?

I looked back to her early education for clues. It was then that I recalled that she had struggled on standardized tests during elementary school. I remembered that she had scored in a surprisingly low percentile on reading tests. However, because I am not a micromanaging parent, I thought, *Well, she's coming in with low scores, but she is smart and seems happy, and I know not every aspect of intelligence develops concurrently, so let's just see what happens.* Plus, the school had pulled her out of the classroom, given her additional services, evaluated her reading skills and determined they were fine, and then put her back in with her standard reading class. At the time, this confirmed my thought that the test score was an anomaly, even though these pull-outs and push-ins occurred year after year.

By the end of Alexa's sophomore year, the situation had become terrible. She was up until two o'clock every morning working on homework, yet she continued to be overwhelmed. That is when I actually grew worried about her self-confidence. She had started to talk about herself openly in self-deprecating and diminishing ways. Beyond that, I didn't know how she would have time to prepare for and take the tests to get into college because even day-to-day homework was overwhelming.

We tried medication for ADHD, but it did not make a significant difference; we hired tutors, but nothing really worked—she was already so focused and organized. The summer after her sophomore year, confused and at a loss as to why nothing I had tried was helping her and the school system hadn't identified any learning issues, I took her to get private neuropsychological testing. Maybe the school system and I were both missing something? At the end of the testing process, the neuropsychologist met with Alexa and me. She told us that "Alexa has a hardwired reading disability. Her reading comprehension is far below grade level, and it is sheer determination, compensatory strategies, and willpower that have kept her grades at the level they're at, especially given the fact that she doesn't truly understand much of what she's reading." She said that Alexa, now a junior in high school, was reading at a seventh-grade level. She turned to my daughter and asked her what strategies she had been using to get her through school with so little comprehension. Alexa explained her techniques, which, albeit impressive, were also burdensome. They had worked, but at great cost to her self-worth, sleep, and conceptual understanding.

After receiving this staggering information, I came to understand that Alexa's brain was not hardwired for inferencing, reaching conclusions based on evidence and reasoning, and had almost no neuroplasticity in this region. Inferencing is required in all types of reading, not just reading for school-work or entertainment, but even in word problems in math or comprehending maps.

Fortunately, the neuropsychologist had a positive outlook. She told me, "Your daughter is a fighter. She has built these remarkable compensatory strategies, annotating everything she reads, trying to make sense of it. Yet, this process takes an inordinate amount of time and doesn't help her synthesize material, which is what would be required on an exam. In addition, her processing speed of the material she's reading is slow, making timed tests a particularly poor indicator of her knowledge."

And my daughter had never complained about any of it! An unfortunate characteristic she inherited from me.

Alexa was actually relieved by the results the tests showed us. The information began to topple misconceptions and assumptions she had hidden about her intellectual inferiority. At last, there was a potential explanation for her struggles, as well as decisions we could make and actions we could take to do something about it. Reading remediation and more time could help her. She felt hopeful about the possibilities, and because she clearly was not daunted by hard work, reading remediation did not seem to bother her at all.

Unfortunately, getting the school on board to give her the extra time she needed to process information during tests turned into a battle. The hope we felt for her academic future didn't turn into immediate relief since I needed to involve an attorney to fight the school for this one accommodation, even with the neuropsychologist's findings. The school insisted, "She's really fine. She's getting mostly B's and even some A's." But that was not the point. She was exhausting herself to achieve that.

In a fascinating turn of events, the school's attorney took our side, noting, "The mother is only asking for extra time; give her the extra time. The poor girl is working until two in the morning. What's the big deal?" Under duress, the school complied.

Yes, Alexa's performance overall improved with remediation and extra time, but more importantly, her confidence began to build steadily as the effort it took to complete schoolwork started to ease. She went from seeing herself as less intelligent to viewing herself as equal to her peers. Her persistence in working on improving her reading with remediation and practice was clear, but so was her defiance in rejecting what she considered to be easier ways that were offered to her to solve her reading problems.

This is not to say that these other ways to solve the reading problem were wrong; they were just not right for her and for the way she wanted to view herself. She was offered and advised to use audiobooks instead of learning to read independently, and she was offered and advised to use note takers instead of reading or looking at smartboards and taking notes simultaneously. She rejected both of these ideas immediately. She set a challenge for herself to learn to read from a book and take notes like everyone else because she "believed" she could learn to do it, despite the disability, and no one was going to tell her otherwise. It was like when she was smaller and wanted to learn to do a handstand in the pool: she practiced from sunup to sundown until she could do it.

I often joke how everything seems to happen easily for Steven, and Alexa has to work for it, but because of that, who knows? In the end, success may come more easily to her because she *never*, ever gives up. And *that* is so much better than fleeting happiness!

I have seen this in my daughter in so many ways since that diagnosis. She scored far higher than anyone predicted on the high school standardized tests because she went into them with the attitude of "I am going to beat this test. I do not care how many times I have to take it; I am going to figure out a way. I'm smart enough to do it!" And she did.

Then, she set her sights on a college that was a high reach and incredibly challenging academically, but she got in! She fought to learn to read instead of using audiobooks, and after mastering becoming a note taker, she now takes notes for other college students! Presently, she has her sights set on a doctorate in psychology. I have no doubt that if this continues to be her goal, she will succeed because she does not *forecast negative assumptions* or *focus on pleasing people*, and once she *makes a decision*, she *faces her fears* and *closes* whatever she finds *personally rewarding* to her. She resiliently defies anyone who doesn't believe in her!

I learn so much from my daughter. She epitomizes defiant resilience. She may embody it inherently, but luckily for most of us, it is a skill that can also be learned by using the tools of Sustainable Life Satisfaction.

Make sure your defiance is authentic—that it's *yours.*

What makes the resilience that contributes to Sustainable Life Satisfaction *defiant* is the ability to curate information from the outside world and select from that information those things that feel authentic to us—so that the decision we make is autonomous and true to ourselves and does not stem from the desire to people please, delegate, or opinion-shop.

For example, for me, even if a doctor tells me to stay home and rest for a few days after an illness or a surgery, I know that staying home and feeling like a patient is not the best way for me to heal. That may be the best way for *most* people to heal, but that is not the best way for *me*. I listen to the doctors and hear what they're saying, filter that through my knowledge of myself, and then choose to use or discard the information I am receiving from that source, even if the source is reputable. In that way, my choice is defiant because I am not just "going along" with a source that supposedly has more knowledge than I do because of age, experience, a position of authority, or education—I am filtering information through my knowledge of myself and then taking action, even though to many people, that action appears to be defiant.

And then comes resilience—cultural, inherent, and adaptive resilience....

Resilience can be defined as how we respond to adversity. One path to resilience is found in *cultural resilience*. This can be the result of generations of grit—like groups of people who live and thrive despite having come through difficult circumstances for generations, such as harsh climates or economic hardships. It can also apply to people who survive trauma and pass their faith in survival on to their offspring and future generations. I recently heard about some early research indicating that people whose family members had been transparent with them about traumatic events in their past and shared that information tended to raise more resilient children than those who sheltered their children from the truths of their traumas. This brings us back to social learning theory because these parents are models of overcoming adversity instead of burying it under shame or anxiety. As Daniel Siegel, coauthor with Tina Payne Bryson of *The Yes Brain*, put it in a March 28, 2018, interview with *The New York Times*, "A parent's resilience serves as a template for a child to see how to deal with challenges, how to understand their own emotions."

Of course, there are going to be many other contributing factors to something as complex as a cultural predisposition to resilience, but ultimately, knowing and believing that your parent has coped with, managed, and overcome something challenging or awful and is still strong, handling life, and even thriving serves as a model for resilience in a meaningful way—resilient parents raise resilient children. They are definitely modeling things like problem-solving, coping, feelings of effectiveness in the world, and internal locus of control—all while they are avoiding assumptions and facing fears. These are fundamental qualities that speak to resilience. In contrast, the children who do not know that their parents have been through adversity never have a model for it. There is never a discussion, and the parents end up rescuing or (even worse) ignoring their children instead of fostering resilience, which results in the opposite of cultural resilience—a generation that does not know how to handle trauma and, as a result, will have a much longer and arduous path to travel toward resilience.

Psychiatrist and concentration camp survivor Viktor Frankl is perhaps the ultimate example of this. He used the trauma he endured to inspire and guide generations toward resilience. As he so eloquently put it, "Fundamentally, therefore, any man can, even under such circumstances, decide what shall become of him—mentally and spiritually. He may retain his human dignity even in a concentration camp. Dostoevsky said once, 'There is only one thing that I dread: not to be worthy of my sufferings.' These words frequently came to my mind after I became acquainted with those martyrs whose behavior in camp, whose suffering and death, bore witness to the fact that the last inner freedom cannot be lost. It can be said that they were worthy of their sufferings; the way they bore their suffering was a genuine inner achievement. It is this spiritual freedom—which cannot be taken away—that makes life meaningful and purposeful."

There is also considerable psychological research on people who are *inherently* resilient, like Alexa, who come to their resilience naturally—they are born with it or develop and retain it early in their childhoods and are then able to draw on it as they mature. People like this just seem to *know* how to be resilient. It is a rare trait, so most of us need the opportunity to learn how to be resilient instead of hoping we were born with inherent resiliency.

The third type of resilience is *adaptive*. As the Sustainable Life Satisfaction steps show us, adaptative resilience can be cultivated, like Steven did when he walked through fear to play baseball. People like Steven *learn* resilience and how to overcome challenges and obstacles. The Sustainable Life Satisfaction techniques do just that: teach resilience. By avoiding assumptions and reducing people-pleasing behaviors, you can more effectively face your fears, make decisions, and close on those decisions. Active self-reinforcement sustains this journey toward a lifetime of satisfaction. It is these techniques that yield a more formidable version of you, one with improved self-confidence, self-worth, self-respect, self-efficacy, and feelings of inherent lovability. Within that empowered self-concept, you will find your resilience.

Of course, adaptive resilience can also be augmented and sustained by inherent resilience, and, as with any human quality, there is a spectrum. However, if you look at what resilient people have in common, you will see—as the outcomes of my Sustainable Life Satisfaction strategies show—that you can arrive at resilience by either the adaptative path or by way of the inherent path, as long as you learn to and continue to take action.

So, whether we set out on the path to resilience through being culturally, inherently, or adaptively resilient, we all have the capacity to arrive there! *Because* we all have the capacity to become resilient *and* we all have the capacity to become authentically defiant, we can build on these traits to reach a place of agency, where we're flourishing on our own terms—where we live a life beyond happiness!

Over the years, I have admired people who I think personify defiant resilience....

They have a strong belief in their lovability and exhibit self-confidence, self-efficacy, self-respect, and self-worth despite the many challenges and obstacles they have faced: my children, of course, and all the people whose stories I have shared with you. But some of my heroes aren't my clients or my family but people, either living or deceased, who have truly inspired me. My rather eclectic list includes Louisa May Alcott, Tyler Perry, Queen Elizabeth I, Coco Chanel, Michael J. Fox, Ruth Bader Ginsburg, and Oprah Winfrey, as well as many social justice advocates and athletes who have overcome tremendous obstacles and embodied defiant resilience.

Each of them overcame adversity, challenged social norms, and broke down barriers. The characteristics they share include being authentic, passionate, driven, and inspiring, with an empowered self-concept and an almost tangible self-efficacy. In pursuing their goals, they cared about the people they loved and humans in general but did not let what naysayers said or thought about them dampen their desire to fulfill their dreams, thus embodying interdependence without codependence. They all maintained hope, strength, and positivity throughout significant adversity—all characteristics of Sustainable Life Satisfaction.

I think we need to apply social learning theory to what these heroes model as we increase our sense of personal power in our everyday lives and focus on what we can control. Here are some of the common qualities I have seen in my heroes who embody resilience:

- They are self-reliant, self-assured, self-possessed people who feel they have good problem-solving skills.
- They feel effective in the world and are confident in their self-worth.
- They do not feel worried about being judged, controlled, or criticized by others regarding their decisions.
- They do not seek reassurance or validation; they have an internal locus of control.

And you can become more like them when you:

- Manage negative, hopeless thoughts: stop negative forecasting.

- Curate information from outside of yourself: keep or discard opinions, regardless of the source, depending on what feels authentic to you.
- Do not look to the outside world for the reinforcement and reassurance of your worth.
- Practice your problem-solving skills. This will enhance your belief in your ability to bounce back during times of adversity.
- Embrace challenges as opportunities for growth in your coping ability.
- Believe in your right to be true to your authenticity, drive, passions, and inspirations—don't doubt.
- Reduce your negativity bias and focus on what is going well in your life—this will help to strengthen your resolve, hope, and positivity during times of adversity.
- Do not let people's perceptions of you dampen your desire to fulfill your dreams.
- Embody the qualities of Sustainable Life Satisfaction (avoid assumptions, stop people pleasing, face your fears, make decisions, close, and self-reinforce).
- Remember that hope, love, and defiant resilience run deep within all of us.

There's one more hero I need to talk about....

Before I conclude, I want to tell you about my remarkable and inspiring client Rena. I met her when she was in her early thirties. As a toddler, Rena was in a serious car accident and barely survived, and as a result, she lived with severely diminished mobility on the right side of her body. Remarkably, she suffered no head injury, and her cognitive abilities remained intact—she was incredibly intelligent. Both she and her mother were later diagnosed with serious and persistent mental illness. Her twin sister has not been diagnosed, but I am fairly certain that she, too, has a serious and persistent mental illness.

When I met Rena, she was riddled with fears that prevented her from living the life she wanted. She was scared to drive. She had gone to college on the West Coast, had been physically assaulted, had dropped out, and now did not want to go back to college. She could not imagine ever getting married, even though she would have liked to someday. She lived with her parents and had a tough time picturing herself ever moving out and living on her own. Despite how smart she was, she had extraordinarily little agency in her own life. Rena was really struggling when I met her.

As I have recommended throughout this presentation of the Sustainable Life Satisfaction model, we broke each struggle of hers down into clearly defined, bite-size tasks. We started with driving....

Although she was terrified to drive, she was willing to take incremental steps toward it. First, I employed a cutting-edge technique called "eye movement desensitization and reprocessing," or EMDR, which helped her process and work through the conscious *and* unconscious traumatic memories of the car crash. The second step was to talk with her parents about purchasing a modified car. Once she had the car, she had to practice for both her written test and her driving test. She applied herself to both of these tasks, and she passed both tests with flying colors. The sense of efficacy and confidence Rena gained from learning how to drive emboldened her to tackle other major life struggles.

Next on the list was college. Again, we broke it down into steps: coming up with a viable list of schools, taking the requisite tests, completing the applications. She got accepted to most of the places she applied to, and she decided that this time around, she would attend a state school she could commute to from Manhattan. Her parents wanted her to choose a major that would be less challenging because they were worried about her physical limitations and wanted her to focus on managing her mental health issues; however, Rena recognized that this was not her parents' education—it was hers—so she decided to major in art history.

She embraced academia because of her love of art history and endeavored to apply for a prestigious PhD program; she succeeded not only in closing on the process of completing the application but also in being accepted! She is currently pursuing her dream of becoming an art history professor one day. Rena's family was concerned about the financial implications of the debt involved in a PhD program, as well the physical and mental strain it might place on her, yet, still, she was not deterred. She was confident in her decision to pursue her passion despite the hurdles she might face. She was no longer working to please them; she was working to sustain and please herself.

As for romance, during a high school reunion, she became reacquainted with a former classmate of hers, someone with whom she had been too reserved and shy to communicate when she was a teenager. She was not sure initially if she wanted to dually focus on her education and a relationship, and she rejected his advances. However, he was undeterred. Once she felt she had her footing in school and could refocus her attention on a relationship, Rena was able to shift her attention to this acquaintance. She had known that focusing on too many large life events at one time could lead to a deterioration not only in her overall life satisfaction, but also in her mental health status because of her challenges in being "present" in multiple areas at one time. But her self-assuredness that she could pursue the relationship on her terms at a time that made the most practical sense to her—instead of rushing into something before she was ready—demonstrated self-control and self-love. She came to find out later that her new love interest had been impressed by her self-awareness. In Rena's case, the waiting was worth it, and now they are engaged.

Rena is a remarkable person. I have so much admiration for her. Here is a young woman with a history of multiple traumatic events who thrives with both physical and mental health challenges. She has caring but opinionated and overbearing parents who can be quick to make negative assumptions about her future plans. This is a challenging set of circumstances. Rena's success in life is surely a testament to her strength of character. And her defiant resilience is likewise a testament to the efficacy of the six Sustainable Life Satisfaction techniques. Let's think about how they apply to her....

She avoided assumptions.

When I met Rena, she assumed that because of her disability, many of the things she wanted in life—to drive, to have a respectable job, to have a satisfying love life—were beyond her grasp. She had to recognize that these were assumptions that were holding her back from having the kind of life she wanted.

She didn't people please.
Learning that her satisfaction was more important than pleasing her parents, and might ultimately please them as well, was a huge accomplishment. She recognized that she was becoming angry and resentful when thinking about living the life they wanted for her, instead of pursuing her dreams, despite her desire to please them.

She faced her fears.
All the financial risks she has taken were scary for Rena: learning to drive and buying a car, going back to school and taking out loans to pay for a degree of which her parents were not in favor.

She made decisions and stuck to them.
After having received a bachelor's degree in art history, it was not easy for Rena to defy her parents' wishes and pursue a doctorate. But she made the decision anyway. And she chose to wait to embark on a relationship despite being pursued.

Rena was a closer.
Taking the series of steps to drive a car and following through was closing. So was the series of steps required to go back to college and then to graduate school.

She remembered to self-reinforce.
Rena has a number of go-to self-reinforcement strategies. She recently rescued a cat. Playing with her new pet is something that brings her a lot of joy. Also, she is artistic in her own right, so she likes to do what she calls "trash-basket multimedia projects." When she completes a challenging

task or faces a fear, she'll go to the items she's collected that had been discarded by herself or her friends and turn them into collages. She always keeps a box of discarded items ready to be turned into art.

When you have reached the point, as Rena has, where you are comfortable *not* assuming, *not* people pleasing, facing your fears, making decisions, and closing tasks, you have installed a pretty reliable internal compass. You are comfortable listening to your inner voice and setting goals based on your own desires rather than on what's conventional or popular or what your parents, teachers, or even children want you to do.

There is no question that Rena has faced adversity in her life and yet here she is: engaged, in graduate school, confident in her dealings with other people, making fabulous art in her spare time, and dreaming about an achievable future.

There is a clear correlation between Rena's ability to overcome internal and external obstacles to achieve her goals and her capacity to thrive despite the blows that life has delivered to her. Each challenge she faced, each action she successfully undertook, added to the psychic armor with which she met the next challenge in her life.

Closer that I am, I want to leave you with my definition of defiant resilience—the key to a life of sustainable satisfaction.

I see it as "the ability to spring back from adversity with a newfound belief in your ability to face challenges with renewed hope, strength, and positivity." I believe that we all have the power and strength to possess defiant resilience. Defiant resilience is the ability to challenge the "It's not possible" or the "No, I can't" and change them to "It *is* possible" or "Yes, I can," even if it seems to defy the odds. It is the ability to believe in yourself and your capabilities even when others may not or when it's outside of the norm. It is continuing to try to get into graduate school after receiving multiple rejections year after year, taking a career path that feels meaningful to you and ignoring the naysayers, learning to drive and head off on a path of independence despite a disability, finding a doctor who believes there is a medical issue with your child despite being rebuffed by experts. Defiant resilience is learning to read without an audiobook and not letting a missed boat ruin a vacation. It's loving yourself even when people sabotage your self-worth; it's enjoying your own company and having faith in your own agency; it's standing up against a system that may be stacked against you.

Above all, I want to stress that the defiant resilience path of Sustainable Life Satisfaction is a journey, and the goal is the process, *not* the feeling. Success is self-acceptance and self-love, which may mean that there are certain skills you will struggle to master as you sustainably increase your awareness of them. There will be days when you will feel more resilient and days when you will feel less so—that is part of the human condition. We are people, not robots. Accept this truth and look at your overall improvement. This doesn't necessarily mean you will never take steps back, but the journey does keep moving forward.

No one can be inoculated against adversity—it is part of the human condition. But learning to trust in your ability to solve problem after problem as they arise feeds your ability to spring back from adverse situations with hope, positivity, and renewed strength. Sustainable Life Satisfaction means not giving in to despair, because you know you have a well of strength to draw on. It means that when life tells you, "You can't do this," you can respond, "With all due respect, I know what I am capable of, and yes, I can!" Take it from me: I *am certain* you can!

Six Core Techniques of Sustainable Life Satisfaction

ONE: *Avoid assumptions....*

By avoiding assumptions, you can learn to have agency in any situation *instead* of taking action based on what you imagine other people are thinking or feeling about you. Instead, your actions are based on reliable evidence.

TWO: *Reduce people-pleasing behaviors....*

What I mean by "people-pleasing behaviors" is subordinating and conforming your needs, desires, wishes, and dreams to what other people think they should be—or to what you *imagine* others want them to be. This technique of consciously not defaulting to putting the needs and desires of others ahead of your own enables you to live an authentic life.

THREE: *Face your fears....*

The purpose of the facing-fears technique is not to stop you from feeling afraid—after all, some fear is healthy—it is to train you not to let your fears prevent you from working toward and achieving your goals. You can learn to use your fears as a positive motivation that propels you to move toward the life you want, resulting in more self-efficacy and self-respect.

FOUR: *Make decisions....*

Using this technique, you will liberate yourself to make choices by recognizing that almost every decision we settle on is, at best, just a well-informed guess and that there are almost no decisions that cannot be reversed. Of course, there are a few exceptions—like having a child or a financial gamble that results in an irrevocable loss—but when it comes to the day-to-day, most decisions—like which college to go to or whether to move to a new city—can be undone. The point is to take action and *make* a decision.

FIVE: *Acknowledge that starting is easy, but closing is hard....*

This truism teaches the skill of following through and completing tasks, from small ones that will make your life easier—like folding and putting away laundry or paying your bills on time—to large ones that can change your life—like starting a new business, buying a home, or ending a destructive relationship. Following through on what we start, *no matter* how difficult the process, will lead to self-confidence, self-efficacy, and self-respect.

Six: *Self-reinforce by rewarding yourself....*

This enables you to stay on the path to belief in your inherent lovability. As you consistently provide yourself with tangible rewards for successfully executing any of the other five techniques, you will make the cognitive shift from aspiring to gain and needing praise, rewards, and reassurance from others to appreciating the profound value of giving those things to yourself.

Key Terms

All-or-none thinking. Thinking in superlatives—applying words like "always," "never," "best," or "worst," either to describe yourself or your situation to other people or even to yourself.

Codependence. An imbalanced overreliance on people or forces outside oneself to affirm or acknowledge one's behavior, value, or emotions.

Cognitive-behavioral therapy. The branch of psychology that was developed to target and correct thinking errors, to address people's eroded self-worth, self-confidence, self-efficacy, and self-respect. The synthesis of behavioral and cognitive therapies, it was conceived by Dr. Aaron T. Beck, a psychiatrist at the University of Pennsylvania in the 1960s.

Defiant resilience. The ability to spring back from adversity with an energy fueled by self-generated positivity and hope that allows you to expand your sense of purpose and act on it. The culmination of Sustainable Life Satisfaction.

Interdependence. A way to describe a healthy relationship between two people wherein the impact of external factors on the internal locus of control is balanced. The opposite of interdependence is codependency.

Intermittent reinforcement. Inconsistent or occasional rewards that may act to increase a negative, damaging, or undesirable behavior instead of extinguishing it.

Locus of control. The degree to which we believe that we—as opposed to external forces beyond our influence—have agency over the outcome of events in our lives.

Magnification. Magnification is making a small, negative event very big in your mind; it is blowing something minor completely out of proportion to the reality of the situation.

Minimization. Ignoring or mentally reducing the significance of positive events or feedback.

Mood modulation. The reduction of the intensity of an emotional reaction, bringing it into sensible or realistic proportion with the severity or gravity of an event, relationship, or situation.

Negative forecasting. Fortune-telling; predicting and expecting terrible things to happen and dwelling on those predictions.

Neuroplasticity. The ability of the brain to create, strengthen, and reorganize synaptic connections between nerve cells, especially as the result of learning. ("Neurons that fire together wire together.")

Positive psychology. The scientific study of well-being and happiness, proponents of which include Martin Seligman, who is often referred to as the "father" of positive psychology.

Reinforcement. The act of encouraging or cementing a pattern of behavior or thought, especially by way of reward or punishment.

Satisfaction. Being content in body, mind, and situation. It comes with the feeling of fulfillment we have when we arrive at or are in the process of executing something we want to do, as well as with the pleasure we receive from achieving the expectations that we have for ourselves.

Self-actualization. Defined by Abraham Maslow as "the desire for self-fulfillment, namely, to the tendency for him to become actualized in what he is potentially. This tendency might be phrased as the desire to become more and more what one is, to become everything that one is capable of becoming."

Self-concept. Who we think we are. It contains the Five Elements of Empowered Life:

Self-Worth

Self-Confidence

Self-Efficacy

Self-Respect

Belief in Your Inherent Lovability

Self-efficacy. Confidence in your problem-solving and coping skills, and in your overall competence to manage life's challenges, even if it means opposing, redirecting, or changing learned and reinforced beliefs and behavior. This term also originated with Bandura.

Social Learning Theory. Developed by psychologist Albert Bandura, who posited that we learn from each other via imitation, modeling, and observation and adjust our behaviors and reactions as they are reinforced, especially by our caregivers during childhood.

Thinking errors. When our thoughts do not match up with the reality of a situation or experience; cognitive distortions.

Acknowledgments

This book would not have been possible without the love, support, and encouragement from my children: Steven and Alexa. They have challenged me to face the fears of mother-hood—both holding on and letting go. I have watched them have a hand in molding the person I have become and as a result shifted the trajectory of my life in a remarkable direction! I have no doubt their fingerprints are all over Sustainable Life Satis-faction. I am in awe of their patience as I talked through ideas and asked them to read and reread versions of chapters for their commendable insights.

Thanks to everyone at Post Hill Press for taking a leap of faith and believing in me and this book. Special thanks to Madeline Sturgeon for her guidance and thoughtful suggestions throughout the editing process.

I owe a debt of gratitude to Ramon Hervey for being the first person to stand behind Sustainable Life Satisfaction as an idea worth pursuing. Whenever I need encouragement, he is there, and I can always count on him for honesty and transparency, which has built a trusting and lasting partnership.

ACKNOWLEDGMENTS

This book would not have been possible were it not for Michael Palgon. He saw the bigger picture and how people could benefit from a book about Sustainable Life Satisfaction when others could not.

Writing a book that maintains one's voice without sounding pedantic is a daunting task. I am indebted to the editorial help, insight, and support of Alice Peck for helping me maintain a sense of approachability through the written word. Thank you as well to Crystal Sershen for her discerning eye.

To Eva Feindler, who saw something in me others had not. She was the first to challenge me and teach me to face my fears head-on, testing the limits of my competence. She taught me about support without rescuing and how to believe in myself.

There are a few people who are responsible for who I have become but are no longer with me to see this book published. I owe them a debt of gratitude that I cannot repay. My father and maternal grandmother had hands in shaping who I am and what Sustainable Life Satisfaction is. I hope within it they would have found some aspects of what they taught me and know those lessons will live on.

A shout-out to my social media and branding team: Andrea Grant, Matt Ogilvie, Katherine Peterson, Bridget Stangland, Connor Misset, James Weber, Susan Stangland, and Mike Ruiz. Without you, no one would have ever heard of Sustainable Life Satisfaction.

Finally, to those who have been there all along to boost me up. You are all the best: Lisa Lombardi, Wendy Levine, Guy Philoche, Amy Scher, Debbie Jacobson, Judy McCoy, Brunald Bejko, all the members of the "HQ" group (you know who you are), and my many wonderful clients throughout the years.

Bibliography

Bandura, Albert. *Psychological Modeling: Conflicting Theories.* United Kingdom: Transaction Publishers, 2017.

Bandura, Albert. *Self-Efficacy in Changing Societies.* United Kingdom: Cambridge University Press, 1997.

Bandura, Albert. *Social Foundations of Thought and Action: A Social Cognitive Theory.* United Kingdom: Prentice-Hall, 1986.

Beattie, Melody. *Codependent No More: How to Stop Controlling Others and Start Caring for Yourself.* United States: Hazelden Publishing, 2009.

Braiker, Harriet. *The Disease to Please: Curing the People-Pleasing Syndrome.* United States: McGraw-Hill Education, 2002.

Chapman University Survey on American Fears. *The Chapman University Survey on American Fears | The Earl Babbie Research Center | Chapman University,* www.chapman.edu/wilkinson/research-centers/babbie-center/survey-american-fears.aspx.

Csikszentmihalyi, Mihaly. *Flow: The Psychology of Optimal Experience.* New York: Harper & Row, 1990.

Eskelinen, Matti, and Paula Ollonen. "Assessment of 'Cancer-Prone Personality' Characteristics in Healthy Study Subjects and in Patients with Breast Disease and Breast Cancer Using the Commitment Questionnaire: A Prospective Case–Control Study in Finland." *Anticancer Research* 31, no. 11 (November 2011): 4013-4017.

Ecton, Randolph B., and Eva L. Feindler. *Adolescent Anger Control: Cognitive-Behavioral Techniques.* United Kingdom: Pergamon Press, 1986.

Feindler, Eva L., and Grace R. Kalfus. *Adolescent Behavior Therapy Handbook.* United States: Springer Publishing Company, 1990.

Frankl, Viktor. *Man's Search for Meaning.* New York: Washington Square Press, 1984.

Hopkins, Ellen. "Susan Sontag Lightens Up." *Los Angeles Times,* August 16, 1992.

James, Ian A., and Katherine Kendell. "Unfinished Processing in the Emotional Disorders: The Zeigarnik Effect." *Behavioural and Cognitive Psychotherapy* 25, no. 4 (1997): 329-337.

Kaufman, Scott Barry. *Transcend: The New Science of Self-Actualization.* United States: Penguin Publishing Group, 2021.

Kendall, Stephen B. "Preference for Intermittent Reinforcement." *Journal of the Experimental Analysis of Behavior* 21, no. 3 (May 1974): 463-473.

Kindlon, Daniel J. *Too Much of a Good Thing: Raising Children of Character in an Indulgent Age.* United States: Miramax Books, 2003.

Kushner, Robert F., and Seung W. Choi. "Prevalence of Unhealthy Lifestyle Patterns Among Overweight and Obese Adults." *Obesity* 18, no. 6 (October 2009): 1160-1167. DOI: 10.1038/oby.2009.376.

Lally, Phillippa, Cornelia H. M. van Jaarsveld, Henry W. W. Potts, and Jane Wardle. "How Are Habits Formed: Modeling Habit Formation in the Real World." *European Journal of Social Psychology* 40, no. 6 (October 2010). DOI: 10.1002/ejsp.674.

Lamott, Anne. "There's a whole chapter on perfectionism in Bird by Bird, because it is the great enemy of the writer, and of life, our sweet messy beautiful screwed up human lives." Facebook, May 12, 2014. https://www.facebook.com/AnneLamott/posts/theres-a-whole-chapter-on-perfectionism-in-bird-by-bird-because-it-is-the-great-/485327514930230/.

Langford, Joe, and Pauline Rose Clance. "The Imposter Phenomenon: Recent Research Findings Regarding Dynamics, Personality, and Family Patterns and Their Implications for Treatment." *Psychotherapy: Theory, Research, Practice, Training* 30, no. 3 (1993): 495-501.

LeCroy, Craig W. *Handbook of Child and Adolescent Treatment Manuals*. United States: Lexington Books, 1994.

Levine, Madeline. *Teach Your Children Well: Why Values and Coping Skills Matter More Than Grades, Trophies, Or "Fat Envelopes."* United Kingdom: Harper, 2012.

Lorde, Audre. *A Burst of Light: And Other Essays*. United States: Dover Publications, 2017.

Maslow, Abraham H. *Motivation and Personality*. United States: Harper & Row, 1981.

Masters, John C., Thomas G. Burish, Steven D. Hollon, and David C. Rimm. *Behavior Therapy: Techniques and Empirical Findings*. United Kingdom: Harcourt Brace Jovanovich, 1987.

Maté, Gabor. *When the Body Says No: The Cost of Hidden Stress*. United States: Knopf Canada, 2011.

Mook, Douglas G. *Motivation: The Organization of Action*. United Kingdom: W.W. Norton, 1996.

Obama, Michelle. "'Hardball with Chris Matthews' for Feb. 12." NBC News, February 13, 2007, www.nbcnews.com/id/wbna17131614.

Pear, Joseph J., and Garry Martin. *Behavior Modification: What It Is and How to Do It.* United Kingdom: Taylor & Francis, 2015.

Polya, G., and John H. Conway. *How to Solve It: A New Aspect of Mathematical Method.* United Kingdom: Princeton University Press, 2014.

Popek, Emily F. "To Raise Resilient Kids, Be a Resilient Parent." *The New York Times*, March 28, 2018, www.nytimes.com/2018 /03/28/well/family/to-raise-resilient-kids-be-a-resilient- parent.html.

Rymarczyk, Karolina, Anna Turbacz, Włodzimierz Strus, and Jan Cieciuch. "Type C Personality: Conceptual Refinement and Preliminary Operationalization." *Frontiers in Psychology* 11 (2020).

Satir, Virginia. *The New Peoplemaking.* United States: Science and Behavior Books, 1988.

Siegel, Daniel J., and Tina Payne Bryson. *The Yes Brain: How to Cultivate Courage, Curiosity, and Resilience in Your Child.* Bantam, 2019.

Seligman, Martin E. P. *Authentic Happiness: Using the New Positive Psychology to Realize Your Potential for Lasting Fulfillment.* United Kingdom: Free Press, 2002. Page 13.

Sifferlin, Alexandra. "How Gratitude Helps You Become More Patient." *Time*, April 4, 2016, time.com/4277661/gratitude- patience-self-control/.

Solso, Robert L., Otto H. MacLin, and M. Kimberly MacLin. *Cognitive Psychology.* United Kingdom: Pearson/Allyn and Bacon, 2008.

Southwick, Steven M., and Dennis S. Charney. *Resilience: The Science of Mastering Life's Greatest Challenges.* United Kingdom: Cambridge University Press, 2018.

van der Weiden, Anouk, Jeroen Benjamins, Marleen Gillebaart, Jan Fekke Ybema, and Denise de Ridder. "How to Form Good Habits? A Longitudinal Field Study on the Role of Self-Control in Habit Formation." *Frontiers in Psychology* 11 (2020): 560.

Van Lange, Paul A. M., and Daniel Balliet. "Interdependence Theory." American Psychological Association, 2014. DOI:10.4135/9781446201022.n39.

Wansink, Brian, and Jeffery Sobal. "Mindless Eating: The 200 Daily Food Decisions We Overlook." *Environment and Behavior* 39, no. 1 (January 2007): 106–123. DOI: 10.1177/0013916506295573.